Donnini's
PASTA

TIBERIO DONNINI
GIANNI MILANI
PETER PIERCE

VIKING O'NEIL

Viking O'Neil
Penguin Books Australia Ltd
487 Maroondah Highway, PO Box 257
Ringwood, Victoria, 3134, Australia
Penguin Books Ltd
Harmondsworth, Middlesex, England
Viking Penguin Inc.
40 West 23rd Street, New York, N.Y. 10010, U.S.A.
Penguin Books Canada Limited
2801 John Street, Markham, Ontario, Canada L3R 1B4
Penguin Books (N.Z.) Ltd
182-190 Wairau Road, Auckland 10, New Zealand

First published by Thomas Nelson Australia 1984
This edition published by Penguin Books Australia Ltd 1988
Copyright © Tiberio Donnini, Gianni Milani, Peter Pierce 1988

Produced by Viking O'Neil
56 Claremont Street, South Yarra, Victoria 3141, Australia
A division of Penguin Books Australia Ltd

Illustrations by Lorraine Ellis
Design by Leonie Stott
Typeset by Meredith Typesetting
Printed and bound by Australian Print Group

National Library of Australia
Cataloguing in Publication Data

Donnini, Tiberio
  Donnini's pasta.

  Rev. and expanded ed.
  Includes index.
  ISBN 0 670 90118 0.
  I. Cookery (Macaroni). I. Milani, Gianni.
  II. Pierce, Peter. III. Title.

641.8′22

To Marco, Gianna, Riccardo, Giulia, Matia, Lisa and
Catherine

CONTENTS

PREFACE

Donnini's Pasta Book is special among the Italian cook books available in Australia, because it has grown out of a long tradition of pasta cooking and eating in my family, both here and in Italy. It presents an unrivalled number of recipes for sauces to accompany pasta of all shapes, sizes and colours. This is its main object. We want readers and cooks to enjoy our recipes because we want to give back some of the pleasure that we get from cooking and eating pasta. Some recipe books talk about the delights of food so stiffly that they give no sense at all of the pleasures of eating, let alone of cooking; they are as enticing as making love by proxy. Not so *Donnini's Pasta Book*: we want to give you an appetite as you follow or challenge our recipes and make your own variations on them. So, please, use the book — write on it, argue about the recipes and the comments that you find here.

As well as the recipes for *pasta in brodo* (pasta with soup), *risotto* and for *pasta asciutta* (so called 'dry' pasta which is used with sauces), and answers to any problems which you may encounter when cooking, we advise you how to make pasta in your own home and how to cook it well. We have also included a description of various pastas. My friend, Peter Pierce — who knows about such things — has supplied information essential for anyone interested in pasta and the place of this great food in literature and legend. I am better at the cooking; he is better at writing; it's a toss-up which of us is the better pasta eater. Peter also mentions some of the disputes that this best behaved and most amiable of foods has provoked and gives some history of the ways in which Italian cooking has been adapted in Australia.

Ours are family recipes and our advice about how to make your own pasta and the different sauces to accompany it rests on generations of experience in Italy and in our own restaurants and shops here. We are based in Melbourne, but we hope that our book will be welcomed throughout Australia. Italian cooking is enjoyed everywhere now, but it is not generally realized that a real appreciation of the place of pasta in *cucina Italiana* is only a recent development in Australia.

Besides its practical features, *Donnini's Pasta Book* is written in praise of a food that we love to eat: a wholesome, flexible, nourishing and delicious food. Put it another way — kids love it, and as they grow up they still do. Pasta also has the undeniable advantage these days of being economical to make or to buy. The sauces described here range from the simplest, quickest and cheapest (not only vegetable sauces — you will find one made from breadcrumbs) to the richest and most complex. Recipes for seafood sauces and sauces made from meat, game and poultry are all here.

If pasta is a new experience for you, we hope that *Donnini's Pasta Book* will be the start of a love affair. If you are already in love, congratulations.

Tiberio Donnini

INTRODUCTION

PASTA IN HISTORY

The diversity of cooking in the Italian peninsula is because it was the scene of successive waves of migration, some peaceful, others violent, over thousands of years. First came the Etruscans, then the Greeks, then the Romans. From these occupations of the land developed the seminal cooking style of Europe. This *cucina Italiana* is a style of great adaptability, one that has shown itself capable of colonising not only Europe, but much of the world. One of the many arts of Italian cooking is the knack of substituting one ingredient for another, subtly and economically to vary a recipe. The results are striking: wheat soup is transformed into bean soup, or barley soup into tomato soup. Remember also that, crucial as the tomato is in modern Italian cooking, it was not widely used until about the sixteenth century. Sometimes Italian cooking is described as poor, *povero*, but this is a word that only signifies the enormous respect that the inhabitants of the peninsula have had for meat and expensive spices. Coupled with that respect, was a determination to ignore as few usable ingredients as possible. Yet this common sense has given another cuisine a propaganda advantage that is undeserved.

In many circles, French cuisine is regarded as paramount. Consider its classic dishes — *crêpes suzette, canard à l'orange, pâté de foie gras*. Yet *crespelle Fiorentine* were invented before the French crêpes. One of the earliest of all cooking books, *L'anonimo Toscano*, published in the fourteenth century, reports a recipe for duck in orange sauce — a duck stuffed with apple and coated with the juice of oranges. Everyone knows, after all, the historical importance of the ducks and geese whose cackling once saved Rome, and which also served to keep streets and courts clean by their relentless, omnivorous appetites. Recipes for duck and goose liver paste were published in the cookbook of Bartolomeo

1

Sacchi, *Platina*, in 1475, and in Massiburgo's cookbook of 1549. A recipe for puff pastry, Florentine style, occurs as early as the fourteenth century. The sweet tooth of the Italians derives from pre-Roman and Roman times, when figs, honey, fruit juices, whipped cream and jam came to be used widely. However it was not until the Middle Ages that sweets became a specialty of cooking in the cities. In the south fruit predominated, in the north, sweet biscuits were made rich with butter and yeast.

But, as our title suggests, we are primarily concerned in this book with pasta. Throughout the Mediterranean basin the mixture of flour and water has long been known to man, whether it was for the making of pitta bread, or pizza, or *focaccia* (a cake, or bun). The best breadmakers in Republican and Imperial Rome were reckoned to be the Greeks. There are many tales to explain why in some parts of the Italian peninsula the bread is not salted. Some say that this was because of the high tax on salt, others stress the scarcity of the product, but the real reason is that bread without salt absorbs less humidity, becomes less soggy, hence can be preserved longer. The origin of the making of pasta dough is lost in distant time, even though one can be sure that the mixture of flour and water which we have been discussing, must have led the Mediterranean people by short steps to the making of pasta.

There is no agreement about when pasta was introduced to Italy, or by whom. Several sources reckon that the Ostrogoths brought it with them from Eastern Europe when they invaded Italy in the fifth century AD. Certainly this explanation suited some twentieth-century antagonists of pasta, who argued that a barbarous food (as they regarded it) must have had barbarian origins. Another theory contends that pasta originated in Asia, where noodles have for so many centuries been part of cooking. Specifically, no less a person than Marco Polo (1254-1324), the Venetian adventurer and entrepreneur, has been credited with introducing pasta to Italy along with news of other, less tangible wonders. It may of course be that he reintroduced or popularized a kind of food which was already known to Italians. Some evidence suggests that pasta was eaten in Etruscan times.

Despite frequent references to pasta in literature and in legend, its more recent career is not easily plotted.

In Boccaccio's *Decameron* (1349-53), the poet imagines the mythical country of Bengodi, where there is a mountain of grated *Parmigiano* cheese, on top of which dwell people who do nothing but make *maccheroni* and *ravioli*. It was not until the first half of the sixteenth century that the tomato (which is used more often than any other ingredient in making sauces for pasta) was introduced into Europe from the New World. In the same period, the chefs of Catherine de Medici were dressing pasta with honey, butter, sugar, saffron and cinnamon. In the seventeenth century, the Neapolitans were reputedly the world's champion pasta eaters. Some apparently could gorge themselves with six pounds of *maccheroni* taken in one long gobble, shovelled into the mouth with both hands.

Guiseppe di Lampedusa's famous novel, *The Leopard*, gives a more edifying picture of the enjoyment of pasta in Sicily in 1860. The Prince, a cosmopolitan himself, knowing that his Sicilian dinner companions would regard a first course of soup as insipid, organizes his servants to bring to table a giant silver dish containing a *maccheroni* pie:

> The burnished gold of the crusts, the fragrance of sugar and cinnamon they exuded, were but preludes to the delights released from the interior when the knife broke the crust; first came a spice-laden haze, then chicken livers, hard-boiled eggs, sliced ham, chicken and truffles in masses of piping hot, glistening macaroni, to which the meat juice gave an exquisite hue of suede.

Such feasting is rarer now, when pasta is eaten more simply if with no less relish.

While the literary evidence of how pasta came to be made in Italy in so many different shapes and with such a variety of sauces is fragmented, it is easier to trace its dissemination to other countries. In Restoration (that is, late seventeenth-century) England, there was a vogue for things Italian. Pasta became an expensive imported delicacy. Somewhat later — in the mid eighteenth century — 'macaroni' came in slang usage to mean fop or dandy. The association came from the Macaroni Club, a group of rich young men who had originally assembled because of their love of foreign cooking.

3

Such a mis-use of the word suggests accurately that pasta, and the art of cooking it, were not altogether intelligently appreciated in England. The culinary custom was to soak pasta for long periods before it was cooked. For example, in 1792 an anonymous guide to good cooking recommended that before pasta was ready for English palates, it needed three hours' boiling in water, fifteen minutes' cooking in broth, and then mixing with bread in a soup tureen!

In the USA in the eighteenth century, the Revolutionary War song 'Yankee Doodle' (composed by Edward Bangs some time around 1775) made its famous though incomprehensible reference to sticking a feather in the cap and calling it macaroni. Thomas Jefferson — later to be President of the USA — imported poplars from Lombardy, Tuscan wines and also a machine for making *spaghetti*. Extensive Italian migration to America, and with it the large-scale introduction of pasta to American palates, began late in the nineteenth century.

By the twentieth century, pasta was coming under some surprising and virulent attacks. When Marinetti (1876-1944), the founder of Futurism, attacked pasta in public in 1930, he did so not out of a local aversion to the food, but as part of his Futurist political progamme, which called for the discarding of past traditions and the creation of new forms of expression that exalted modern technology, speed, violence and war. Marinetti thought that pasta was conducive to none of these things. His war against it was ranged on a bewildering number of fronts: he attacked its nutritional, moral, aesthetic, sexual and nationalistic failings. Marinetti contended that pasta was an obsolete food that encouraged the worst qualities of the Italian people, among them indolence and lack of virility. In consequence, there was violent argument about pasta in Italy; a passion was shown towards food that no other nation could have equalled. The argument has by now been won: there are no loud complaints about the capabilities of Italians or Australians who love to eat pasta and the recommendation of pasta by people such as Luciano Pavarotti on one end of the weight scale and jockeys at the other, suggests that while pasta is undoubtedly nutritious, and a delight to see and to eat, it need not be fattening.

The history of pasta has dramatic and mysterious moments, but the more important part of its story involves the developments — across many centuries — in the art and craft of pasta cooking. Thus we can trace the regional styles that grew up in Italy, the incorporation of new ingredients, the proliferation of idiosyncratic shapes and colours of pasta. The recipe section of *Donnini's Pasta Book* provides some background to these regional differences and developments and it demonstrates that the history of pasta cooking is the history of individual cooks and regions. Pasta cooking supremely expresses individuality: cooks who begin with the simplest of ingredients produce marvellously varied fare.

Among other things, *Donnini's Pasta Book* is an invitation to readers to contribute their part to the history of pasta in Australia where so many people are coming freshly to its temptations.

ITALIAN COOKING IN AUSTRALIA

In *The Watcher on the Cast Iron Balcony*, the first volume of his autobiographical trilogy, Hal Porter reminisces about one of the earliest Italian restaurants in Melbourne, one which still thrives — the Cafe Latin. It was there in 1928 that Porter first became acquainted with the cosmopolitan delights of wine drinking, a different cuisine, the sound (macaronic, we could say) of many European languages and the pleasures of conversation. The coming of Italian cooking to Australia and the broadening of Australian culture were firmly related in Porter's mind. Yet in his recollection of what he ate in the Latin, there is no mention of pasta. The menu, as Porter recalls it, was a much more limited one than that of many good Italian restaurants in Australia today.

Both the Cafe Latin and the Society Restaurant were established in Melbourne by the late 1920s. They represented an important advance in the quality of food available in the city, but they remained virtually the only Italian restaurants for two decades. The change came with post-war migration to Australia. Fortunately, many Italian migrants insisted on importing their traditional, regional

5

cuisines, principally to their homes, but also to the growing number of restaurants in the larger cities of Australia. From the early 1950s, one sign of their arrival was the coffee machines which began to appear in cafes and restaurants. Other kinds of ambience (for example, pseudo-Mexican decor) gave way to one that was approximately Italian. These cafes became regular meeting places for the many young, unmarried men who had recently left Italy. It was in the early 1950s that the Cafe Sport opened in inner-urban Carlton. The University Cafe, run by Tiberio Donnini's grandparents, opened in 1952.

The original cafe consisted of a restaurant downstairs and a billiard room upstairs. This reflected its function as one of the first places in Melbourne where young Italian migrants (most of them men at this stage) could meet and enjoy good, inexpensive, home-style food in surroundings which were nostalgic for all those reasons. Later, when the quality of the food and the friendly atmosphere of the cafe became more widely known, and a more varied clientele began to frequent it, the restaurant area was moved upstairs and a coffee bar installed below. The same arrangement still obtains.

Since the early 1950s, Lygon Street in Carlton has become Australia's 'Little Italy'. It is crowded with Italian shops and shopkeepers — with a variety of delicatessens, *pasticceri*, *gelaterie*, coffee shops and restaurants. The Italian effects have sometimes been more calculated than authentic. Nevertheless, Lygon Street is the small part of one Australian city where something closest to European urban life — lived out of doors, sociably, noisily — has come into being. Here, in Lygon Street, the advantages of Italian migration and Australian climate have most happily met.

Unfortunately, the quality of restaurants in this predominantly Italian-Australian street has varied a lot. Italians were not, of course, to blame for such inventive local horrors as the cold *spaghetti* sandwich which many an Australian child took as his or her school lunch in the 1950s. However, in the first decade after the end of the Second World War, standards of Italian cooking were lowered in an attempt to adapt to the as yet unsophisticated Australian palates. From the early 1960s, *pizza* houses began to open.

Toto's in Lygon Street was the first of these and the first establishment of this kind in Australia. The irony of this change was that *pizza* — a Neopolitan snack — achieved a prominence in Australia that it has never enjoyed on restaurant menus in Italy. In other restaurants, cooks assumed that Australians would share the English penchant for *spaghetti Bolognese* and for anything labelled *Parmigiana*. Again, neither sauce is common — let alone triumphant — on restaurant menus in Italy. In the 1970s, there was a fashion in Lygon Street for fish restaurants with Italian names. One of their staples was *spaghetti marinara*. Here the irony is that splendid local ingredients were being put to an inauthentic use: in Italy *spaghetti marinara* traditionally contains no seafood at all, as you will see when you come to the Donnini recipe for it in the *pasta asciutta* section.

Many of these post-war Italian restaurants in Australia were opened by ex-waiters who had little training in Italian cooking. Their menus were depressingly similar and unvarying. The attempt to please at the expense of authenticity was paramount. In many cases, Italian cooking was bastardized before it became acclimatized. Even today — when the general level is the highest that it has ever been — it could be argued that there is still no first-class Italian restaurant in Australia. None, that is, comparable to a restaurant of the highest quality in Italy. For those of you who will be lucky enough to travel to Italy in the near future, we have inserted particulars of a dozen of the finest restaurants in various cities of Italy. You can read about their special dishes and enjoy the mouth-watering anticipation of what we hope will be visits to them.

There are three grades of restaurants in Italy, and this distinction has not been clearly established among many of the purportedly Italian restaurants in Australia. The simplest kind of restaurant is the *osteria*, which offers one or two cheap courses (that is, something like the old-fashioned, unelaborate and unpretentious counter lunch). Then there is the *trattoria*, which offers a larger, but fixed range of courses. In fact, the customer is given what the restaurant wants to cook: his or her choice is limited, but more attention can thereby be given to perfecting the dishes which are offered.

Finally comes the *ristorante*, offering a much more comprehensive and ambitious menu, and preparing other dishes at the customer's request.

Donnini's is more like a *trattoria*. A principal feature is *tris di pasta Donnini* — the offer of three pasta dishes at the start of the meal. This choice of pasta dishes gives customers the opportunity to taste different sauces and to try different shapes of pasta, in a rich combination of flavours. No other recent innovation has had such an influence on the general scene of Italian cooking in Melbourne, where the practice of offering the mixed pasta has been widely adopted. In consequence, many more people are learning about the variety of pasta, its adaptability and the pleasures of eating it.

Donnini's has sought and in some measure succeeded in creating a demand for a different kind of Italian restaurant in Australia— one which educates the tastes of its patrons by providing authentic recipes and by showing respect for the culinary traditions and the regional differences behind those recipes. At the same time, the restaurant has benefited from the willingness of Australians to join in the communal delights of Italian cooking, and from the superiority of many Australian ingredients. For instance, seafood is not only of high quality, but it is available fresh all the year round. Meat is also excellent, although pork products — especially sausages and *prosciutto* — still have some way to go to catch up to Italian standards. The availability and relatively low cost of Australian vegetables has also been helpful as many recipes for sauces show.

Tiberio Donnini and his family have sought to establish the custom of eating and enjoying food which has been cooked to genuine Italian recipes. It could perhaps be viewed as one of the best kinds of multi-cultural exchange.

Peter Pierce

EATING IN ITALY

As promised we have provided a short list of excellent restaurants from the many thousands of that quality in Italy. This will be a guide to those of you visiting Italy as to where to find great places to eat, what you can expect to pay and the food and wine that you can expect to savour.

Ristorante San Domenico, Imola. 40026 (Bologna) Via Sacchi 1, Phone 0542.29000, closed on Monday.
Cost per person $85 to $100. Seats 45, must book.

This is one of the finest of northern Italian restaurants, where — from the comprehensive menu — only the best food will be found. Signor Morini treats his guests as friends, despite the outstanding reputation of his restaurant. A visit there will be a highlight of your trip to Italy.

Ristorante Grassilli, Bologna 40125.
Via del Luzzo 3, Phone 051.222961, closed on Wednesday and in August.
Cost per person $40 to $50. Seats 35, must book.

This restaurant is next door to the Two Towers in Bologna. Specialties of the house include *fagiolini della casa* (a bean stew), *gnocchi verdi al gorgonzola, filetti all'acetto di champagne, arresto di maiale* (loin of pork) and many regional specialties of Bologna. Excellent local wines complement the food.

La Cantinetta Antinori, Firenze 50100
Piazza Antinori, Phone 055.292234, closed on
Saturday and Sunday.
Cost per person $40 to $50. Seats 70, must book.

In this most elegant restaurant you should always commence your meal with an aperitif of Antinori Champagne Brut. Favoured dishes include *il pinzimonio di verduna, zuppa di cipolla* (for which you will find Donnini's recipe on p.69), *vitello tonato* (veal in tuna sauce), *gallinella al vino* (the fabled dish of little birds that Italians love), *tripa, fagioli al olio, pane nero abrustolito* (black bread toasted with very fine oil). For sweets try the *crostata di pesche* and the *biscotti di prado.*

Enoteca Pinchiorri, Firenze 50100
Via Gibellina 87, Phone 055.263653, closed on
Monday.
Cost per person $60 to $70. Seats 50, must book.

This is a very long established Florentine restaurant in a fifteenth century building. The dishes from its very progressive and perfectionist kitchen are light and tasty and vary according to what is offering in the market. An excellent range of French and Italian wines is available here.

Ristorante La Scaletta, Milano 20144.
Piazzo Stazione di Porta Nuova, Phone 02.8350290.
Closed Monday and Sunday and from 20 to 30
April and 24 December to 7 January.
Cost per person $60 to $80. Seats 30, must book.

This is an elegant restaurant with sublime food, whose
specialties include *gnocchetti con la zucca* (dumplings
with pumpkin), rice with nettles and strawberries,
fillets of beef with marrow sauce, veal kidneys with
mushrooms. The sweets are exquisite if you can
manage them at the end of the meal.

Ristorante Bagutta, Milano 20121.
Via Bagutta 14, Phone 02.702767.
Closed Sunday and from 7 to 31 August and from
23 December to 7 January.
Cost per person $40 to $50. Seats 150, no booking
required.

This restaurant is famous not only for the excellence
of its food but for the international literary prize which
its owners offer. Specialties include *fettucine del
tartufo, risotto al zapperana, cotolette alla Milanese.*
There is always excellent fresh fish here.

Ristorante dell'Amelia alla Giustizia, Mestre Venezia 30171.
Via Miranese, Phone 041.913951.
Closed on Wednesday and from 15 September to 15 October.
Cost per person $40 to $50. Seats 200, no booking required.

This restaurant, only ten kilometres from the centre of Venice, offers traditional food in a rustic atmosphere. All kinds of fish are good here, but remember that for Venetians the smallest fish are always preferred. Specialties of the house include *baccala*, chicken livers in typical Venetian style and crabmeat. Pasta is also outstanding.

Ristorante La Colomba, Venezia 30124.
Piscina di Frezzeria, Phone 041.23817.
Closed on Tuesday and from 7 November to 17 December.
Cost per person $40 to $50. Seats 100.

Just behind St Mark's Square, this is a typical Venetian restaurant, with its large and conspicuous menu. *Pesce al cartoccio* is one specialty, as is *risi e bisi* (rice with beans). There is a delicious assortment of sweets in this — a restaurant steeped in local folklore.

Ristorante Girarrosto Fiorentino, Roma 00100
(behind the USA Embassy)
Via Sicilia 40, Phone 06.460660. Closed on Friday.
Cost per person $35 to $40. Seats 70, must book.

The kitchen and dining room of this restaurant are divided by a glass partition which enables you to see your food being prepared. Recommended dishes are *ribollita* (re-boiled soup), *pasta e fagioli* (a bean soup), *lasagnette al prosciutto, spaghetti alla campagnola, fiorentina* (T-bone steak), *stracotto* (roast yearling beef), *coniglio in tega* (rabbit). Excellent local and Tuscan wines are served.

Ristorante Coriolano, Roma 00100.
Via Ancona 14, Phone 06.8449501. Closed on
Sunday and during August.
Cost per person $35 to $50. Seats 60, must book.

This is a classical and elegant restaurant with a superb wine list. Its specialties include terrine of rice, *fettucine alla Romana, zuppa di fagioli, capretto* (kid), *involtini alla Romana, vitellone al Barolo.*

Ristorante Zeffirino, Genova 16121
Via XX Settembre 20, Phone 010.591990. Closed
on Wednesday.
Cost per person $30 to $45. Seats 150.

This restaurant is run by the Belloni family, in
particular by the sons of the original proprietor. It
specialises in pasta, veal and fish. The cuisine is
classical and simple and the restaurant is a watering
hole for many famous people.

Ristorante Fini, Modena 41100
Piazzale San Francesco, Phone 059.223314
Closed on Thursday and from 1 to 25 August.
Cost per person $30 to $40. Seats 150, no booking
required.

This is the best restaurant in Modena, whose
specialties are *tortellini*, white *lasagna* with
mushrooms, and boiled meats in various sauces. From
an excellent list of wines be sure to try the Lambrusco
Fini. The proprietor, Dr G. Fini, is one of the greatest
promoters abroad of the gastronomic excellence of
Italy.

MAKING AND COOKING PASTA

HINTS FOR BEGINNERS

In the words of James Beard 'you need never be at a loss for something good to eat if you have some pasta and the resources of an ordinary kitchen'.

One of the joys of preparing pasta is that it never ceases to stimulate one's imagination. The aim of this book, like all cookery books, is to stimulate, to guide, certainly, but mostly to encourage and urge the reader on to bigger and better culinary adventures. Never feel that you must follow any of the recipes *exactly*. We would like you to improvise, to indulge your fantasies, to adapt the recipes to what you have available in the pantry or garden.

Pasta, apart from being fun to make and wonderful to eat, is, of course, very economical and nutritious. Very few of the recipes in this collection contain expensive ingredients. In most cases if you buy sensibly — for example use vegetables that are in season rather than scarce — you can produce a much cheaper and more nutritious meal than with any other form of cooking. There is no waste in this style of cooking either: the meat that makes the broth can be eaten sauced as a main course; any leftovers can make meatballs, or the filling for *cannelloni*, and so on.

In Australia, pasta is available to us in three different forms: commercially packaged dried pasta, shop-made partially dried pasta, and fresh home-made pasta. The latter, of course, is more time consuming to make but more economical and enjoyable. Fresh pasta is a quite different eating experience to dried pasta and certainly an experience not to be missed but enjoyed as frequently as possible.

The best flour for making pasta is that called *semolina*, which is ground from the endosperm or heart of durum wheat. Durum wheat contains more of the protein gluten than ordinary flour, and it is the gluten component that gives dough elasticity and tension. Pasta is best made from a mixture of this flour and water or a mixture of plain flour with eggs. The recipes in this book use eggs.

Ideally, flour made from durum wheat should be used for pasta made at home. However, even though much of it is grown in this country, it is very difficult to obtain. We suggest that you buy any well-known brand of plain flour for making pasta at home, but take every possible step to ensure its freshness. It is a good policy never to buy large quantities of flour unless you are sure you can use it quickly. Always buy flour from a large supermarket, not the corner store where the stock may be old.

Shop-made pasta, such as that sold at Donnini's, is available in a variety of sizes and shapes, not so varied as that made for commercial packaging but greater than you are probably prepared to make at home. Any of the plain pasta, purchased fresh, can be successfully dried for storing. Only filled pasta, such as *ravioli*, *tortellini* and *cannelloni*, can be frozen, and this should be done as soon as it is bought or made.

MAKING PASTA AT HOME

In preparing this recipe for pasta we have tried to make it useful and practical for the greatest number of Australian cooks. Unfortunately, something we do not have in most modern kitchens is that luxurious commodity — space — and unfortunately, to make pasta in the traditional fashion one does need space, and lots of it. Accordingly, we recommend two major diversions from the traditional method.

First, we suggest that the dough be mixed in a large bowl rather than directly on the work surface. Should you wish to mix the dough in the traditional way follow the directions exactly as given but place the flour directly on the work surface. We would advise against using a food processor to mix the dough.

Second, the purchase of a pasta-rolling machine is also advisable. There are several brands available in most department stores and good Italian hardware shops. They range in price from $30 to $50. Certainly, pasta can be rolled by hand, but again it requires a large uncluttered work space and a special rolling-pin — smaller in diameter than the conventional rolling-pin and ideally measuring in length the cook's height from floor to waist. You can work with a shorter rolling-pin but it will require much more energy on your part.

Should you wish to roll the dough by hand, place the dough on a well-floured surface, flatten it, and start rolling from the centre out to the edge, turning the dough as you roll it to keep a circular shape of even thickness. Make sure that the dough does not stick to the work surface; if this does happen loosen the dough and dust the work surface with more flour. Keep rolling the dough in this fashion until it is about ½ centimetre thick. The next stage involves pulling and stretching the dough as opposed to rolling it. Curl the far end of the circle around the rolling-pin and roll it up halfway towards you; quickly roll it back and forth and at the same time move your hands lightly back and forth along the length of the rolling-pin to stretch the dough. Keep turning the dough and repeating this process until the pasta dough is paper thin and has a transparent quality. The dough should be of an even colour — any dark patches indicate areas of thickness.

After the dough has rested for approximately thirty minutes, it can be cut. To prepare it for cutting into whatever pasta you want, fold the dough into a flat roll about 7 centimetres wide. Always use a very sharp knife. If making *tagliatelle*, cut it into ½ to 1 centimetre slices; if making *lasagne* cut it into sheets appropriate for your dish.

BASIC PASTA DOUGH

500 g flour
4 large eggs (65s)

Put the flour into a large bowl. Make a well in the centre of the flour and break the eggs directly into this cavity.

Beat the eggs with a fork inside the well, gradually incorporating the flour. The fork will soon become clogged with dough. Clean it off and continue mixing with your hands until the flour and eggs are well incorporated.

Form the dough into a ball and, still working in the bowl, knead the dough with the heel of your hand, adding an additional sprinkling of flour until you reach a non-stick point. Push your finger into the dough: it should bounce straight out and be quite clean.

Turn the dough out on to a floured surface and knead for ten minutes by pressing it over on to itself, pushing the masses together with the heel of your hand. Knead the dough until it has a definite velvety consistency. Any crusty bits of dough should be discarded — if you try to incorporate them they will cause the pasta to break when you are rolling it out or cutting it.

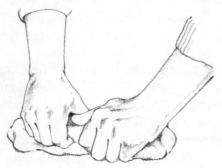

Cover the dough with an inverted bowl or a clean cloth and allow it to rest for thirty minutes.

Attach the pasta machine to your work bench. Make sure that the clamps are firmly in place and that it cannot wobble. *Leave the cutting rollers aside for the moment.* Cut the dough into four equal sections, leaving three of them under the inverted bowl or cloth. Set the machine so that the rollers are at their widest opening. Flatten the piece of dough with the palm of your hand and pass it through the rollers.

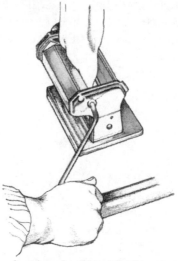

Continue passing the dough through the machine, folding it in half or thirds to fit through, until the dough becomes quite smooth to touch. Start reducing the roller setting as you pass the dough through the machine, until the dough reaches the thickness you require. The dough will now be a long thin sheet of pasta. Lay it on a cloth in an airy place or, better still, hang it over a broom-handle resting securely between two chairs, while you pass the remaining three pieces of dough through the machine. Make sure that the drying pasta is out of the reach of household animals.

The weather determines how long the pasta will need to dry and only experience will be able really to guide you. As a general rule, though, let the pasta dry for fifteen to twenty minutes. The pasta must retain its plasticity. Its texture will be velvety and the sheet will be almost transparent. The pasta is ready to cut when you turn a corner of the sheet back on itself and it does not stick.

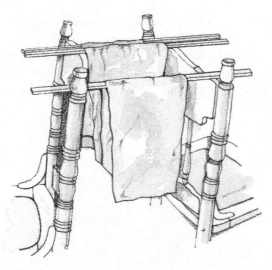

The pasta can be cut into any shape using a knife or the pasta machine. For *lasagne* a knife is the best implement and for *tagliatelle* or *capelli d'angelo* (angel's hair) it is best to use the machine. *Attach the cutting rollers to the pasta machine*, set them to the width required, and pass each sheet of pasta through the rollers. Once you have started cutting a sheet do not stop cranking the machine until the sheet is completely cut, otherwise the pasta strips will break. If the machine does not cut the pasta cleanly, allow the sheet to dry a little longer, but take care that the pasta does not lose its plasticity.

Loosely pick up the strands of pasta and wind them around your fingers into nest-like shapes and put neatly on to a cloth-covered tray for further drying. Once you have cut all the pasta into whatever shapes you require you can cook it straight away, or allow it to dry out completely and store it in air-tight containers.

COLOURING PASTA

Pasta may be coloured with any number of herbs, vegetables or fruits. Once you have mastered the basic technique you will be able to improvise as your fancy and pantry allow.

The traditional colourants are spinach, capsicum, carrot and tomato. As a general rule for ½ kilogram of flour and four eggs, use half an egg-shell of the pre-cooked colourant, e.g. half an eggshell of cooked spinach squeezed dry in a clean cloth will colour the pasta sufficiently. Add the colourant when you add the eggs.

COOKING PASTA

Pasta is easy to cook well. It is also deceptively easy to overcook.

Whether you are cooking fresh or dried pasta it is important to use a large pot. One litre of water for every 100 grams of pasta is a good guide. The proportions can be reduced slightly if you are cooking large quantities: 7 litres should be enough for 1 kilogram of pasta.

Fill the pot with salted water and bring it up to a rolling boil, add all the pasta at once and cook it until it is *al dente*, or firm to the bite. There is no golden rule as to cooking time. The point to remember about home-made pasta is that it cooks very quickly, dried home-made pasta takes a little longer and commercial dried pasta longer still.

Test fresh pasta as soon as it returns to the boil, and every minute thereafter until ready. Commercial pasta can be tested about every four minutes after it returns to the boil, until ready. Once the pasta is *al dente* remove from the heat at once and drain quickly and thoroughly in a large colander.

Whereas in Australia it is general practice to serve the pasta with the sauce placed on top, we advise you to mix the sauce and pasta before it is served. After the pasta is drained, you have a choice of putting the sauce in the empty pot, pouring the drained pasta on top of it and mixing them or of mixing the sauce and pasta on a serving platter.

COLD PASTA

It has become fashionable to serve pasta cold. To do this, cook the pasta in the way described above. When it is *al dente* add a tumbler of iced water to the pot and drain immediately. Cool the pasta under running cold water. Drain thoroughly and toss the pasta in a cold sauce. Never serve cheese with cold pasta. *Salsa di pomodoro al limone* on p.87 is a delicious sauce to serve cold.

WHEN AND HOW MUCH PASTA TO USE

The question of 'how much pasta?' can obviously be answered if you know when you are going to serve the pasta. There are various rules of thumb that can be applied, but probably the best is the commonsense idea of looking at the complete menu for the meal and trying to maintain a good balance overall and within individual courses.

The first course in a traditional Italian meal is almost invariably pasta: either *pasta in brodo*, that is pasta in soup, or *pasta asciutta*, so called 'dry' pasta which is served with sauces. In Australia we often see pasta presented as a main course or as a complete meal in itself, as well as a first course. Certainly, there is nothing wrong with doing this and a bowl of pasta often makes a good luncheon dish followed by an appropriate salad, some fresh fruit and cheese. If you are serving pasta as a first course you will need less than if it is to be a complete meal or a second course. Consideration must also be given to the richness of the pasta sauce and to the courses to precede or follow the pasta.

As a general rule, for *pasta in brodo* you will need approximately 50 grams of pasta per person. For *pasta asciutta* served as a first course 75 to 100 grams per person, and 100 to 150 grams per person if the pasta is a complete meal or second course.

EQUIPMENT FOR MAKING AND COOKING PASTA

Apart from the pasta machine, no unusual appliances or equipment are needed for any of the recipes in this collection. You will need the following equipment.

- A large bowl in which to mix the pasta dough.
- A dough scraper to keep your work surface clean of all clinging particles of dough.
- A pasta rolling and cutting machine. Readily available in Australia, the machine is based on much the same principle as the wringer and is hand cranked. (Electric machines are available but are expensive and not overly reliable.) Always clean the machine with a dry cloth after use, removing any dough or flour which may be stuck in the cutting grooves or rollers with a sharp implement. Never wash the machine.
- A large pot for cooking pasta. You will need a very large pot if you are cooking pasta for a large number. Bear in mind that you will need roughly 1 litre of water for each 100 grams of pasta. Ideally, use one with high sides; this means that the pot is squarely over the heat source and will boil evenly.
- Tongs, for picking up the long pasta. Metal tongs are more practical.
- Wooden spoons.
- A colander. You need a large one. Choose a colander that has a secure, circular base rather than one with legs which can easily topple over.
- Saucepans. These need to be large enough for the soups and sauces.
- Grater for the cheese and nutmeg.
- Lasagne dish. This needs to be deep.

- Ravioli trays (*ravioliera*). It is possible to make *ravioli* without these trays (as explained on p.35). However, they are inexpensive if you decide to purchase them.
- A slotted spoon. This will help you remove without breaking the *gnocchi* as they finish cooking.
- A skimmer to remove excess fat from the broth.

IMPORTANT INGREDIENTS

OLIVE OIL

We recommend that you use olive oil whenever possible. However, if this is not available, maize oil is the most successful alternative. Olive oil comes in a variety of flavour strengths, the strongest being called 'extra virgin'. It must be your own individual taste that guides you in your choice of olive oil. Remember, too, that the nutritional value and flavour of oil is reduced as it cooks, therefore try to start with a minimal amount of oil, adding more at the end of cooking time.

FRESH VEGETABLES AND HERBS

Whenever possible use fresh vegetables and herbs, but only those that are in season and are unblemished and of good quality. It is much better to use good tinned tomatoes, for example, than to buy inferior fresh ones. This may mean that you will only be able to prepare a favourite sauce for a short seasonal period in each year. We have tried to give a comprehensive range of recipes to include all seasonal vegetables, so you can enjoy your food at its prime. Do not settle for second best.

PARSLEY

Continental or curly parsley can be used. Parsley is used in these recipes for flavour, not decoration. That is why it is added at the beginning or middle of the recipes.

GARLIC

There is a common myth that all Italian food contains large quantities of garlic and very little else. There may have been some truth in this argument prior to refrigeration when all foods were of necessity heavily flavoured with spices, garlic or whatever to conceal their lack of freshness. This time, however, has long passed.

You will see that in some recipes the garlic is finely chopped and remains in the sauce, in others it is left whole, skewered diagonally with toothpicks and discarded at the end of cooking. Whichever method is used always remove the two 'eyes' from each end of the garlic by making a 'v' shaped incision with a sharp knife. This stops the garlic repeating.

ONIONS

It is not an exaggeration to suggest that a sauce succeeds or fails on the cooking of the onions. If you undercook them you will not extract the full flavours and these flavours will not develop in the later cooking. So, to obtain the correct flavour from the onions follow closely the directions in the recipe — they have been suggested for very good reasons. For example, onions cooked golden brown give off a sweeter flavour than onions cooked until they are dark brown.

CHEESE

We recommend two particular cheeses in these recipes. The first is *Parmigiano — Reggiano* or *formaggio Parmigiano*. Parmesan is the Australian equivalent of this delicious cheese, but we would suggest that to achieve the authentic flavour of each recipe you should use *Parmigiano*. The second cheese is *pecorino*. Both cheeses are readily available in Australia. They can be used as a table cheese as well as for cooking. Never buy either cheese pre-grated. Always buy only as much as you think you can use and grate it freshly when required. Both cheeses, if wrapped properly, will last for two to three weeks in the refrigerator without coming to harm.

PANCETTA

This is the same cut of pork as bacon, but is cured rather than smoked. It comes rolled in a large sausage shape and is sliced as ordered. *Pancetta* keeps for three weeks in the refrigerator but do not buy too much at once. As with all ingredients it is best to buy only as much as you think you can use.

PROSCIUTTO

This is raw ham cured in a mixture of salt and spices. It is best sliced as fine as tissue paper. As well as the use to which we put it in the following recipes, *prosciutto* is delicious on fresh bread or served with melon and freshly ground black pepper.

VARIETIES OF PASTA AND HOW TO USE THEM

Pasta comes in such an array of shapes and sizes that it can sometimes be difficult to decide which one to use. When making a choice there are two main factors to consider. First, the suitability of the pasta and its capacity to carry, trap or wrap around the sauce being served, and second, given the nature of the sauce, ease of eating. For example, when serving a cream-based sauce, pasta such as *tagliatelle*, pasta with indentations or grooves on it or *gnocchi* are ideal as they catch and carry a lot of the sauce; short curly pastas such as *fusilli* are good for trapping tiny delicacies like the crumbs of the *salsa di mollica de pane* (breadcrumb sauce on p.132); *spaghetti* is good for wrapping around slippery seafoods.

There is no strict rule that you must serve a particular sauce with a particular type of pasta, just use your common sense and your personal preference and the combination will be the right one.

As well as the myriad of shapes and sizes of pasta, the names given to them differ slightly from region to region in Italy. We list those most often used in Australia. The easiest way to describe pasta is to draw it to scale, as we have done overleaf.

It is interesting to note that the word *spaghetti* is derived from *spaghi*, meaning little strings. *Spaghetti* is usually solid and each variation in thickness has a name. For example *capelli d'angelo* is one of the finest, *spaghettini* is thicker than *capelli* but thinner than *spaghetti*. *Spaghetti bucati* is as thick as *spaghetti* but hollow.

Most people aren't aware of the difference between *tagliatelle*, *fettucine* and *pappardelle*. *Tagliatelle* is the flat ribbon of pasta about 8 millimetres wide. *Fettucine* is the same width as *tagliatelle* but thicker. *Pappardelle* is wider than *tagliatelle* but the same thickness. Also, *pappardelle* can be curled at the edges.

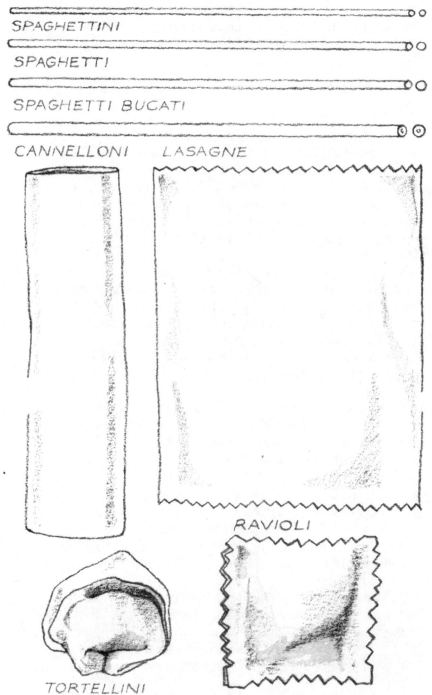

CAPELLI D'ANGELO

SPAGHETTINI

SPAGHETTI

SPAGHETTI BUCATI

CANNELLONI   LASAGNE

RAVIOLI

TORTELLINI

28

TAGLIATELLE

FETTUCCINE

PAPPARDELLE

CURLED PAPPARDELLE

GOMITI   BOMBOLOTTI   CONCHIGLIE

RIGATONI   GRAMIGNA   DITALI

FUSILLI   BUCATINI

QUADRETTI

PENNE

FARFALLE

Short pastas can be solid or hollow. They can also be plain or covered with indentations or lines. The latter, as well as being more attractive, are useful in that the indentations enable them to carry more of the sauce. Short pastas include: *fusilli, penne, rigatoni, bombolotti, maccheroni, farfalle bucatini, conchiglie, ditali, quadretti, gomiti, gramigna.*

The most popular filled pastas are *cannelloni, tortellini, ravioli.* Fillings for these three pastas are limitless: from *ricotta* cheese, to vegetables, to meats, to whatever you may have in the refrigerator.

COOKING TERMS

al dente   firm to the bite

reduce   to boil down a liquid so it is reduced in quantity and concentrated in flavour.

roux   the combination of butter and flour which is the basis of many sauces, such as bechamel.

sauté   to brown food in a small quantity of very hot oil or fat. The oil must be very hot before the food is placed in it to ensure the juices are sealed in.

sweat   to draw the juices from food, usually vegetables. Before major cooking, they are gently cooked in a covered pan in butter or oil until moist and soft, but not coloured.

PASTA TREATS AND SUBSTITUTES

As well as the recipes for *pasta in brodo*, *risotto* and *pasta asciutta*, we are including the recipes for two delicious treats in pasta — *tortellini* and *ripeno di zucca*. Do not be put off by what may appear complicated recipes — the results are well worth the effort.

We are also including the recipes for some traditional substitutes for pasta: *gnocchi*, *polenta*, *passatelli* and *gnoccho*. Not well known in Australia, they are all part of the daily *cucina Italiana*.

Tortellini

There are many weird and entertaining stories about the origins of **tortellini***. They are frequently called Venus' Navels because it is said they were originally formed in their particular shape to honour Venus and her beauty. Another story concerns a chef to a rich nobleman who was having an affair with the nobleman's wife and had created* **tortellini** *in honour of the lady's charms. Even though the nobleman surprised his chef in his wife's bed, he could not dismiss him in fear of losing the maker of the extraordinarily delicious* **tortellini***.*

Perhaps a more practical and likely version is that the **tortellini** *were developed as air-tight packages. In pre-refrigeration times meats and other perishables were wrapped in pasta in much the same way as we now use plastic film or foil. Gradually different shapes, related fillings and methods of preparation evolved.*

Tortellini *looks fiddly and a bother to make. But do not be deterred. Apart from the delicious taste of the finished product, making* **tortellini** *is one of the most satisfying and physically relaxing of all kitchen occupations.*

We offer one recipe for **tortellini***, but do not feel restricted to it.* **Tortellini** *are adaptable and the fillings are as interchangeable as* **ravioli** *fillings.*

Tortellini *are arguably at their best served* **in brodo** *but are also quite delicious and certainly easier to prepare for large numbers served with a cream sauce like* **crema alla Gorgonzola** *on p. 128 or the* **salsa allo stile Modenese** *on p. 138. Remember that whatever filling you choose for your* **tortellini** *it is best* *prepared the day before you make the **tortellini** to allow the fullness of the flavours to develop.*

FILLING
50 g lean pork
50 g lean veal
1 tablespoon butter
3 slices ham
3 slices *mortadella*
3 slices *prosciutto*
50 g poached chicken breast
½ nutmeg, freshly grated
salt
black pepper, freshly ground
150 g *Parmigiano* cheese, freshly grated
2 eggs

Lightly fry the pork and veal in the butter and allow to cool. Put all the remaining ingredients and the cooled meat in the bowl of a food processor and mix to a well-blended paste. Put this mixture aside until you are ready to make the *tortellini*.

PASTA
350 g flour
3 eggs

Make the pasta in exactly the same fashion as for the basic pasta dough on pp. 18-22. This dough will, however, have a very slight stickiness, which will help seal the *tortellini*. There is no necessity to dry the pasta for *tortellini* for the same reason.

Once the dough is properly kneaded cut it into four equal sections, leaving three sections covered with an inverted bowl or plate. Roll the remaining dough through the pasta machine until it is paper thin. The dough can then be cut into rounds with a biscuit cutter or a liqueur glass or it can be cut into 5-centimetre squares with a sharp knife. Place one and a quarter to one and a half teaspoons of the mixture in the centre of each circle or square. Fold the pasta in half and press the edges together to seal the *tortellini*. Turn

the sealed edge back towards the filling edge in a form of cuff, wrap the *tortellini* around your forefinger and press the edges together. Lay the *tortellini* out neatly on a cloth-covered tray. Repeat the remaining three pieces of dough.

The *tortellini* may now be cooked in boiling, salted water or if you are serving them *in brodo*, in that broth. If your *tortellini* are uneven in size make sure that you cook them in batches of even size or put the larger ones on first. The *tortellini* will float to the surface as soon as you put them in the boiling water or broth so this is *not* the test for their being cooked. They will need to cook for eight to ten minutes, but test them before serving.

If you are serving the *tortellini in brodo* allow fifteen per person and serve very hot with plenty of freshly grated *Parmigiano* cheese. Allow twice as many if you are serving them with a sauce.

Ripeno di zucca
Pumpkin ravioli

In most instances the filling for **ravioli** *is suitable for* **tortellini.**
Ravioli *can be made with or without a* **ravioliera** *(a ravioli tray).*

> **FILLING**
> 200 g unpeeled pumpkin (the least watery variety
>   available)
> 100 g *Parmigiano* cheese, freshly grated
> 75 g *amaretti* (Italian macaroons), crushed
> salt
> black pepper, freshly ground

Roast or steam the pumpkin, do not boil it. When the
pumpkin has cooled remove the skin and blend it well with
all the other ingredients. The consistency of the mixture will
depend on the variety and quality of the pumpkin used.
Should the mixture seem too wet (for instance, if the
pumpkin is too watery), add more *Parmigiano* cheese, or if it
is too thick add a little beaten egg.

> **PASTA**
> 350 g flour
> 3 eggs

Make the pasta dough in the usual way as described on
pp. 18-22. If you are making *ravioli* without a *ravioliera*, cut
a large rectangular sheet of pasta and lay it out flat on a
lightly floured board. Place one teaspoon of the filling at
6-centimetre intervals on the sheet. Cover this sheet with a
second sheet of pasta and press it all down firmly. Making
sure there is adequate space to press the edges together to seal
the ravioli air tight, cut around each bump with a sharp knife
or a fluted pastry wheel.

   Alternatively, a *ravioliera* makes the preparation easier.
The *ravioliera* is like a biscuit or madeleine tray, and costs
much the same as these do. Dust the *ravioliera* with a little

flour. Place a sheet of dough on top, a teaspoon of filling on each square and then a further sheet of dough over the top. Roll over the *ravioliera* with a rolling-pin and the serrations on the tray will cut through the pasta, producing neat and even *ravioli*.

The *ravioli* are now ready to be cooked in boiling, salted water. If the *ravioli* are uneven in size make sure that you cook them in batches of even size or put the larger ones on first. The *ravioli* will float to the surface as soon as you put them in the boiling water so this is *not* a test for their being cooked. They will need to cook for eight to ten minutes, but it is best to test them before serving.

The normal serving of *ravioli* is fifteen to twenty pieces per person.

This recipe can also be used to make *tortellini*.

Gnocchi di patate

Potato gnocchi

As this recipe for **gnocchi** *contains no eggs, it is a little more difficult to manage, but the* **gnocchi** *are very fine and never tough or rubbery. The variety of potato used alters the quality of the* **gnocchi**, *as well: a potato high in starch is the most desirable. As a general rule choose large, old, white-skinned potatoes, but, if you can get them, Otway potatoes are ideal. New potatoes and pink skinned potatoes are not suitable.*

> 600 g potatoes, unpeeled
> 150 g flour
> 50 g *Parmigiano* cheese, freshly grated
> 1 dessertspoon salt
> extra flour

Try to choose potatoes that are of an even size. Scrub them free of all soil and leave them whole and unpeeled. This reduces the amount of water they can absorb. Boil the potatoes in salted water, taking care to put the larger ones on first if they are of uneven size. As soon as the potatoes are cooked, drain and peel them while still hot. To protect your hand, hold each potato in a tea towel. Put the potatoes in a large bowl and mash them thoroughly making sure that the mixture is absolutely lump free. Using the masher, incorporate the flour, *Parmigiano* cheese and salt into the potato. The mixture will be sticky but very smooth.

Flour a board and your hands well and turn the dough out on to the board. Knead the dough for five minutes with the heel of your hand, making sure that you constantly fold the dough over on to itself. The dough is ready when it is velvety to the touch. Cut the dough into four equal sections and cover three of these with an inverted plate or bowl. Working on the fourth section, roll the dough into a long sausage shape about 2 centimetres thick. With a sharp knife cut it into 2 centimetre lengths, and then roll each *gnocchi* over the prongs of a fork as illustrated.

This is not decoration but a process first to thin out the middle of the *gnocchi* to enable more even cooking, and second, once the *gnocchi* are cooked the grooves trap particles of sauce, making them even more delicious. Lay the *gnocchi* out neatly on a lightly floured, paper-lined tray. Repeat this procedure with the remaining three pieces of dough.

Before you cook the *gnocchi* make sure you have the sauce you intend to serve with them prepared and hot. All the sauces suggested for pasta are suitable but as *gnocchi* are very absorbent, sauces such as the *pesto alla Genovese* (pp. 92-3) and *crema alla Gorgonzola* (p. 128) are particularly delicious.

Cook the *gnocchi* in a large quantity of boiling salted water. In a short time they will float to the surface which demonstrates they are cooked. If you are preparing *gnocchi* for a large number of people do not be tempted to cook too many at a time. Fifty to sixty in 10 litres of water is about right. As soon as the *gnocchi* are cooked transfer them with a slotted spoon to a heated dish and mask with a little of the sauce you have prepared. Continue with this process until they are all cooked. Add the remainder of the sauce and toss the *gnocchi* gently in it to coat them evenly and thoroughly. Serve with plenty of freshly grated *Parmiagiano* cheese.

If you have made too many *gnocchi* they will keep for up to a week in the refrigerator. Cook them and then cool them completely. Toss them with a little oil in a bowl and cover with a plastic wrap.

Polenta

Polenta has a long and well-loved place in Italy's culinary history developing from an Etruscan staple the Romans later termed **pulmentum.** *It was the forerunner of the Scots' porridge and for some this familiar relation tends to make it a little off putting. But, please, be adventurous!* **Polenta** *is economical as well as rewarding to make, and a most satisfying and delicious dish to eat. It is lighter than pasta and consequently easier to digest. It can be served in an infinite number of ways and in the unlikely event of there being leftovers, these can be fried, grilled or sauced in any way you choose. Do not be deterred by the need to stir the* **polenta** *for one hour; your endeavours are more than repaid by the finished article. Both fine and coarse* **polenta** *are readily available, and although we suggest you use the former to obtain a smoother and more delicate texture, this is purely a matter of personal preference.*

salt
500 ml water
500ml milk
100 g butter
300 g fine ground maize flour

Bring the salted water to the boil in a large pan. Reduce the heat and add the milk and butter. Melt the butter completely. Gradually sprinkle the flour over the surface of the liquid, stirring continuously with a long-handled wooden-spoon and incorporating all the flour. Cook for one hour stirring all the time. You may find it convenient to wrap your hand in a tea towel because, despite the long-handled wooden-spoon, your hand will become hot.

The *polenta* is cooked when it forms a ball-like mass in the saucepan and when you knock the spoon against the rim of the pan the *polenta* falls off cleanly. Turn the *polenta* on to a wooden board. It can be served piping hot at this stage with butter and cheese, as is done traditionally, plain with quail or other game, or any sauce of your choice.

If you wish to use the *polenta* later, while still hot form it into an oblong shape about 2 to 3 centimetres thick. Pat the *polenta* into shape with the back of a metal spoon dipped in cold water. When the *polenta* is cold, cut it into 1 to 2 centimetre slices using a thin wire or a length of thread or dental floss. Slide the wire underneath the *polenta*. Holding the *polenta* on the board firmly with your left hand, the front end of the wire with your right hand cutting cleanly and evenly through the *polenta*.

Once cut it can be covered with *Parmigiano* cheese, baked in the oven for ten minutes, and then devoured with gusto. It can be fried or grilled or served with your favourite pasta sauce. Any leftover *polenta* is particularly delicious for breakfast fried with bacon and eggs.

Polenta alla fontina

Polenta with mountain cheese

> salt
> 500 ml water
> 500 ml milk
> 100 g butter
> 300 g ground maize flour
> 2 cloves garlic, finely chopped
> 200 g *fontina* cheese, melted

Follow the preceding recipe for *polenta* adding the garlic and *fontina* cheese when the *polenta* is almost cooked.

This *polenta* can be eaten unadorned or used in the same variety of ways as plain *polenta*.

Passatelli

Passatelli *are delicious little crouton-like morsels made of eggs,*
Parmigiano *cheese and breadcrumbs. Their shape is produced by*
passing the mixture through a special extruding machine or by hand
cutting. They are cooked and served in broth (see p. 46-8) which
must be of good quality. Do not use tinned consommés or stock
cubes — the result will be disastrous.

The logical second course to follow **passatelli** *is* **bollito**
misto *(mixed boiled meats), which have produced the broth for the*
passatelli, *served with* **salsa verde** *(pp. 165-6). This is a quite*
delicious and filling meal and with care in presentation a very
elegant meal despite the English title of 'mixed boiled meats' and
the institutional kitchen connotations that that carries.

A further advantage, of course, in serving **bollito misto** *is*
the complete lack of waste and the economy that naturally affords.
We would suggest that one chicken and half a kilogram of beef will
produce enough broth and meat for six generous servings with
substantial leftovers of meat and chicken to be minced and used for
the next day's meatballs or **cannelloni.**

> 5 heaped tablespoons breadcrumbs, sieved
> 100 g *Parmigiano* cheese, freshly grated
> 2 tablespoons flour, sieved
> 1/4 teaspoon nutmeg, freshly grated
> 2 eggs

Mix the dry ingredients together in a large bowl. Make a well
in the centre of the mixture and break in the two eggs.
Gradually incorporate the eggs into the mixture with a fork.
The *passatelli* mixture must be firm. If you find that this has
not been achieved, as happens if the eggs are very large,
gradually add a little more cheese or sieved breadcrumbs until
the correct consistency is achieved.

Knead the mixture in the bowl turning the dough over
on to itself with the heel and palm of your hand. Knead for
about five minutes. Turn the mixture out of the bowl and
work again for two to three minutes.

Roll the dough into a pipe shape about 5 centimetres wide. Cut the dough into four equal pieces putting three of the pieces aside for the moment. Roll the dough out thinly and cut into 1-centimetre strips and then into 2-centimetre lengths. Repeat this procedure for the other three pieces of dough. Alternately the dough can be pushed through a special extruding machine which is of course much easier and produces neater and more evenly shaped *passatelli*. However, these machines are difficult to obtain in Australia.

The cut *passatelli* must be used immediately, but if you do not wish to use all the dough, wrap it in foil and refrigerate. It will keep well like this for a few days.

To cook the *passatelli* bring the broth to the boil and maintain over a high heat. Add the *passatelli*. When they come to the surface and the broth returns to the boil they are ready. Serve the *passatelli* in the broth with abundant *Parmigiano* cheese.

Gnocco

Gnocco fritto

Gnocco *are not to be confused with* **gnocchi**, *described on pp. 37-8 These delicious fried pasta shapes are quick and economical to make. Children relish them. They can be used as a filling snack, an accompaniment to a meal, and an unusual cocktail party nibble.*

> **500 g flour**
> **1 tablespoon salt**
> **200 ml milk**
> **250 ml olive oil**

Mix the salt and flour in a large bowl. Form a well in the centre of the flour and add the milk slowly, combining the two with a fork. Now work the dough with your hand to form a coherent mass. Turn out on to a lightly floured board and knead the dough for ten minutes. The best way to do this is to keep rolling the dough over on itself with the palm of your hand. (See diagram on pp. 18-19.)

Form the dough into a sausage shape and cut it into four equal pieces. Knead each segment for five minutes, then form each piece into a flat pattie shape about 10 to 12 centimetres wide and 1 centimetre thick. Cover the dough with an inverted bowl or soup plate and allow to rest for at least five minutes.

Pass the first pattie through the wide roller of your pasta machine ten times and lay it out to dry on a cloth-covered tray. Repeat this process with the remaining pieces of rested dough. Change the machine rollers to number 4 thickness and run each sheet of dough through the machine twice. Put each sheet back on the cloth as you roll. In the order in which you rolled the strips of dough cut them with a sharp knife into any shape you want — triangles, squares, circles, etc.

Prick each shape thoroughly with a fork, making sure that the prongs of the fork fully penetrate the dough. This is the secret to perfect *gnocco* as it allows the oil in which you cook the *gnocco* to penetrate the dough and cook each piece quickly.

Shallow fry the *gnocco* in the olive oil over high heat. They will cook very quickly, puffing up sometimes so much they turn themselves over in the oil. The *gnocco* are cooked when they are puffed and golden brown. Remove them from the oil and drain thoroughly on brown paper or absorbent kitchen paper.

Gnocco are delicious to eat hot and unadorned or you can top them with *prosciutto* or other ham or meats, cheese or, if you have a sweet tooth, jams. *Gnocco* dough may also be prepared enclosing a sweet or savoury filling of your choice. In the former case the cooked *gnocco* can be rolled in castor sugar and cinnamon immediately prior to serving.

Cold, the *gnocco* deflate but are no less delicious. They are good to mop up pasta sauces — particularly *crema alla Gorgonzola* (on p. 128) and any leftovers can be crumbled and served in milk, making a far superior breakfast dish to packaged cereals.

PASTA IN BRODO

Pasta in broth

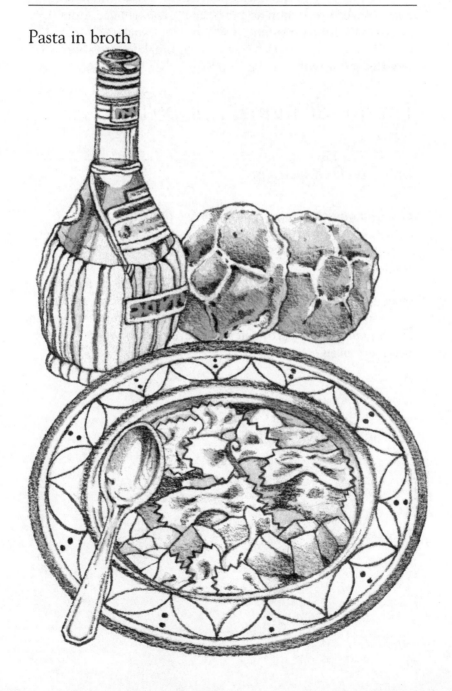

These recipes will serve six to eight people depending not only on their individual appetites but also on the kind of soup — heavy or light, rich or bland.

Allow 50 grams of pasta per person. Any kind of short pasta can be used, such as *quadrettini, ditali, gomiti*, short *maccheroni, penne, rigatoni, fusilli, bucatini, linguini, conchiglie* or, if you only have *spaghetti* to hand, break it into short lengths and it will serve most adequately.

Brodo: di manzo, di pollo, di pesce
Broth: beef, chicken, fish

For the purpose of many of the following recipes these four different flavoured broths may be interchanged at your discretion, though in some cases they should be used as directed for best results.

*In the case of the beef and chicken it is possible to make a main course from these meats after you have used them to make the broth. Two successful and much used accompaniments to them are the **salsa verde cotta** and **salsa verde cruda**, the recipes for which are given on pp. 165-6.*

Brodo di manzo

2-3 sawn marrow bones
2-3 pieces lean beef weighing approx 750 g in total
2 sticks of celery, cut into 7 cm lengths
8-10 whole peppercorns
1 onion, left whole and unpeeled (optional)

Roll and tie each piece of beef securely with kitchen twine. Puncture any tendons at frequent intervals with the point of a sharp knife to tenderize if you intend to use the meat for *bollito misto*. Arrange the bones, beef, vegetables and peppercorns in a large saucepan and cover with water. Bring quickly to a rolling boil, then reduce the heat and boil gently for two to two and a half hours. Carefully remove the meat and reserve for later use. Discard the bones and vegetables and strain the broth several times through a fine sieve lined with kitchen paper until the liquid is quite clear.

If you intend to freeze the broth stand it overnight in the refrigerator to allow any remaining fat to come to the surface from where it may be easily removed.

Brodo di manzo e di pollo

1-2 sawn marrow bones
1-2 pieces of lean beef weighing approx 450 g in total
1 chicken, trussed, plus neck
2 sticks celery, cut into 7 cm lengths
8-10 whole peppercorns
1 onion left whole and unpeeled (optional)

Prepare as for chicken broth.

Brodo di pollo

1 large chicken, trussed, plus neck
2 sticks of celery, cut into 7 cm lengths
8-10 whole peppercorns
2 bay leaves
1 onion left whole and unpeeled (optional)

Arrange the chicken, neck and other ingredients in a large
pot and cover with water. Bring to the boil and cook at a fast
boil for fifteen minutes, reduce the heat and simmer,
covered, for two hours. Carefully remove the chicken and
neck and reserve for later use. Discard the vegetables and
strain the broth several times through a fine sieve lined with
kitchen paper until the liquid is quite clear. If you intend to
freeze the liquid ensure that it is quite free of fat by following
the directions for beef broth.

Brodo di pesce

2 large fish heads and carcasses
2 sticks celery, cut into 8.5 cm lengths
8-10 whole peppercorns
2 bay leaves

Prepare as for chicken broth.

Minestra di fave

Minestrone with broad beans

Broad beans are only available for a short time each year so it is best to make the most of them. This soup is delicious, exploiting the full flavour of broad beans and butter to perfection. Garlic is omitted in this case to enable the two delicate flavours to be enjoyed to their utmost. Try to buy the smallest broad beans you can as these have the best flavour and texture.

100 g butter
1 small onion, finely chopped
1 tablespoon carrot, coarsely grated
1½ sticks of celery, finely chopped
1 tablespoon parsley, finely chopped
500 g fresh broad beans, shelled
2 litres water
salt
black pepper, freshly ground
short pasta (p.46)
Parmigiano cheese, freshly grated

Melt the butter in a large pot. Sweat the onion slowly, making sure that the butter does not burn. Add the carrot, celery and parsley and cook lightly for a few minutes, stirring well to make sure all the ingredients are well coated with butter. Add the broad beans and one or two pods, which can be removed at the end of cooking, but which will strengthen the flavour of the soup. Pour in the water, bring to the boil, reduce the heat and cook covered until the beans are well cooked and a full aroma is developed. Return the soup to the boil, add some short tubular pasta and cook until it is al dente. Add salt to taste. Serve hot with plenty of Parmigiano cheese.

Zuppa di pasta e patate

Potato and pasta soup

This is a soup typical of the central part of Italy. Reminiscent of **minestrone** *it is quicker and more economical to make. The abundance of potato seems to make it a great favourite with children.*

70 g butter
100 ml oil
1 medium onion, finely chopped
1 stick celery, finely chopped
½ carrot, grated
1 tablespoon parsley, finely chopped
600 g potatoes, finely sliced
3 tomatoes, peeled, deseeded and chopped if fresh, or
    6 tomatoes sieved if tinned
salt
black pepper, freshly ground
2 litres beef or chicken broth (pp.46-8)
short pasta (p.46)
Parmigiano cheese, freshly grated

Heat the butter and oil in a large soup pot. Add the onion, celery, carrot and parsley and cook over a medium flame until the onion is golden brown. Add the potatoes and tomatoes and some black pepper. Cover and cook for thirty minutes over medium heat shaking the pot occasionally to prevent the vegetables sticking to it. Add the broth, and salt if necessary. Bring to the boil and add a short pasta, cooking until *al dente*. Serve hot with plenty of *Parmigiano* cheese.

Minestra di zucchini

Zucchini soup

This recipe is a favourite from Cuneo, near Turin, in northern
Italy. In Australia we tend to have zucchini available to us all year
round, the climate being such and the grower's inclinations being
what they are. However, only buy zucchini when they are young
and firm and before the skin has hardened and thickened. Never
use them if they have grown too big. Ideally, a few zucchini plants
grown in the back garden will allow you to enjoy the delights of
these young vegetables only a few inches long. An added bonus is
being able to use the fragile yellow flowers which can be picked
after the zucchini have formed, thereby not harming the plant in
any way. With stem and calyx removed, the flowers can be dipped
in a light batter and fried to a golden brown or they can be stuffed.
Occasionally you can buy fresh young zucchini with their yellow
flowers still attached at the markets or at specialist greengrocers,
however, the flowers wilt quickly so, whether you buy them or
harvest them from your own garden, use them immediately.

100 ml olive oil
1 clove garlic, finely chopped
1 small hot red chilli, carefully deseeded and finely
    chopped
2 kg zucchini, washed and cut into fine rounds
50 g fresh parsley and basil, finely chopped together
black pepper, freshly ground
2 litres water
salt
short pasta (p.46)
Parmigiano cheese, freshly grated

Heat the oil in a large pot and lightly brown the garlic and
chilli. Add the *zucchini* with salt to taste and cook over high
heat for five to six minutes, stirring from time to time to
prevent catching. Lower the heat and add the parsley and
basil and black pepper. Cook for one or two minutes. Add
the water and bring it to the boil. Add the pasta and cook
until *al dente*. If necessary add salt to taste before serving,
with plenty of *Parmigiano* cheese.

51

Passato di verdura all'Italiana

Purée of vegetables

This recipe comes from the Lombardy region of Italy and is a great favourite with children of all ages. It is best served with a short pasta.

> 100 g butter
> 1 small cabbage, finely chopped
> 2 small turnips, finely chopped
> 2 small carrots, finely chopped
> 2 small potatoes, finely chopped
> 1 small bunch spinach, finely chopped
> water
> 2 eggs
> milk
> salt
> black pepper, freshly ground
> short pasta (p.46)

Melt the butter in a large pot and add the vegetables. Cook this slowly for five minutes stirring frequently and taking care that the butter does not burn. Cover them with water. Add salt and pepper to taste, and cook covered until the vegetables are soft. Purée the mixture in a food processor or pass it through a *mouli*. Beat the eggs with a little milk in a warmed soup terrine and add the vegetable purée. Stir well and serve with short pasta which has been cooked *al dente*.

Pasta e piselli

Pasta with pea soup

This Venetian recipe was originally made with the addition of rice rather than pasta. This is equally delicious but tends to thicken the soup rather more than the version below, which is essentially a broth with peas. It is best served with a short pasta.

75 ml olive oil
1 small onion, finely chopped
1 clove garlic, finely chopped
a few basil leaves, finely chopped
300 g fresh peas, shelled
50 g bacon, chopped
1½ litres beef broth (p.47)
500 g tomatoes, peeled and deseeded if fresh, or
    sieved if tinned
salt
black pepper, freshly ground
short pasta (p.46)
Parmigiano cheese, freshly grated

Heat the oil in a large soup pot, add the onion, garlic and basil and very slightly fry until the onion and garlic are a pale golden brown. Add the peas and bacon, stirring well to ensure that all the ingredients are evenly coated with the oil. Pour in the broth together with the tomatoes and salt and pepper to taste. Bring the soup to the boil, cover and simmer for fifteen minutes. Return to the boil and add a short pasta such as *quadrettini*. Cook until *al dente* and serve at once, topped generously with freshly grated *Parmigiano* cheese.

Zuppa alla contadina

Peasant soup

This version of **zuppa alla contadina** *comes from Pavia in the Lombardy region of Italy, and as its name implies it is cheap to make, hearty and filling but certainly none the less delicious.*

> **butter for frying the bread**
> **2 pieces of bread per person**
> **2 eggs per person**
> **250 ml chicken broth per person (p.48)**
> **black pepper, freshly ground**
> ***Parmigiano* cheese, freshly grated**

Heat the butter in a frying pan and lightly fry the slices of bread taking care not to burn the butter. Put the fried bread into individual soup bowls and break the eggs very carefully on to them. Have the chicken broth ready at the boil and then gently ladle it on to the eggs. The heat of the broth will cook the eggs to just the right point of runniness, although, if you prefer, the eggs could be poached separately to make them firmer. Serve at once with freshly grated *Parmigiano* cheese and black pepper.

Crema fredda di patate

Cold cream of potato soup

This soup is usually enjoyed in summer. It is an inexpensive dish from the poorer, mountainous regions of Italy, where the potato is easier to cultivate than most other vegetables.

> 500 g potatoes, thinly sliced
> 4 leeks, thinly sliced
> 1 onion, thinly sliced
> 50 g butter
> 1 tablespoon chives, finely chopped
> ½ teaspoon nutmeg
> 250 g cream
> salt
> pepper
> 1 litre broth (pp.46-8)

Peel the potatoes and slice thinly. Slice the onion and the white part of the leeks thinly also. Cook the vegetables in a pot with butter over a low heat until the onion is transparent. Bring the broth to the boil and add to the vegetables and continue to cook, still over a low heat, for about half an hour. Remove from the heat and strain into a soup tureen. When the soup is quite cool, add the cream, chives, nutmeg, salt and pepper. Refrigerate until needed.

Zuppa al limone

Lemon soup

This soup is a typically Sicilian dish, very quick to make, easily digestible and an unexpected blend of flavours.

> 4 tablespoons rice
> juice of 1 lemon
> 3 eggs
> salt
> 1 litre chicken broth (p.48)

Bring the broth to the boil, add rice and cook for about fifteen minutes. Beat the eggs with the lemon juice and when the rice is nearly cooked, stir this mixture into the broth. Keep stirring on a low heat for a few minutes and then serve.

Minestra di quaglie

Quail soup

During the Italian Renaissance, this dish was very popular in the central and northern parts of Italy. Bread, then more readily and cheaply available than pasta, is used in this delightful and unusual soup.

> **6 quails, cleaned and trussed**
> **6 slices of day old bread**
> **50 g butter**
> **salt**
> **1 litre broth (pp.46-8)**

Clean and truss the quails and put them in a pot with the broth. Bring the broth to the boil and then cook for half an hour over a moderate heat. Remove the quails and keep them warm. Strain the broth and continue to simmer over a low heat. Cut the bread slices in half and cook them in a pan with butter until they are golden on both sides. Place two pieces of bread in each soup bowl and put a quail on top. Add salt to the broth according to taste and ladle the broth, which should have been brought to the boil, over the quails and serve.

Zuppa di basilico

Basil soup

This dish is from the region around Genoa in Liguria, north-western Italy. It is here that the best basil in Italy is produced, with such results as this delightful and aromatic soup.

> 4 medium potatoes, grated
> 2 carrots, grated
> 4 tablespoons basil, finely chopped
> 4 tablespoons *Parmigiano* cheese, freshly grated
> 1 clove garlic, sliced
> 4 slices bread, day old or toasted
> 75 ml olive oil
> 1 litre broth (pp.46-8)
> black pepper, freshly ground

Wash and peel the potatoes and carrots. Grate them. Bring the broth to the boil, add the grated vegetables and cook for ten minutes. Mix the *Parmigiano* and the chopped basil with the olive oil. Rub the slices of bread with the garlic. Place the bread in soup plates, cover with *Parmigiano*, the basil and oil mixture and ladle the broth over it. Top the soup with freshly ground pepper and serve hot.

Zuppa all'erbetta

Herb soup

Of Roman origin, this is one of the oldest soups made in the Emilia-Romagna region and is delicately perfumed with the bouquet of herbs.

4 large potatoes
2 tablespoons butter
oregano, a good pinch
1 tablespoon parsley, finely chopped
1 tablespoon chives, finely chopped
thyme, a pinch
marjoram, a pinch
salt
pepper
1 litre broth (pp.46-8)
4 slices bread, day old or toasted

Peel and grate the potatoes. Cook them in a pot with the butter over a low heat for about ten minutes. Add the thyme, marjoram and oregano, and salt and pepper to taste. Tip the broth over the potatoes and bring it to the boil, then simmer for twenty minutes. At this point sprinkle in the parsley and chives and serve over bread.

Minestrone all'acciuga

Minestrone with anchovies

This is one of those easy and tasty recipes which is known, with some regional variations, throughout Italy.

> 4 anchovy fillets, chopped
> 100 ml olive oil
> 1 clove garlic, chopped
> 1 tablespoon parsley, finely chopped
> 1 cup tinned lentils
> 500 g tomatoes, peeled and deseeded if fresh or
>   sieved if tinned
> 1 litre broth (pp.46-8)
> salt
> pepper
> short pasta, such as *bucatini*

Heat the oil in a pot. Sauté the chopped anchovies and garlic for a few minutes. Add the drained lentils and stir with a wooden spoon. Lower the heat to allow the lentils to absorb the flavour and simmer for a few minutes. Now add the tomatoes, broth, salt and pepper to taste, and bring to the boil. Lower the heat and cook for ten minutes more. Add the pasta and cook for five minutes over a moderate heat. Serve the soup sprinkled with chopped parsley.

Zuppa del'Alto Adige

Soup of the Alto Adige region

The unusual combination of eggs, wine and cinnamon suggests that the soup had its origins in central Europe.

> 4 egg yolks
> 3 glasses dry white wine
> 6 tablespoons cream
> cinnamon, a few pinches
> 8 slices bread, cut in squares
> 1½ litres meat broth (p.47)

Mix the broth, egg yolks, wine, cream and a pinch of cinnamon together. Heat the mixture and stir frequently without letting it boil. Serve very hot with cinnamon-flavoured croutons, fried in butter while the soup has been cooking.

Consommé con le uove

Consommé with eggs

This dish, from the Lombardy region, is very light and satisfying and is enriched by the use of the eggs.

> 4 eggs
> 4 tablespoons sherry, or dry white wine
> 4 tablespoons parsley, chopped
> 1 litre broth (pp.46-8)

Boil the eggs for approximately five minutes. Gently shell them and put one in each soup bowl. Ladle the boiling broth over the eggs and add a tablespoon of sherry or wine and of parsley to each bowl.

Zuppa di Trippa alla Veneta

Tripe soup Venetian style

This is another venerable dish from Venice, especially to be
enjoyed in the wintertime. Cautious eaters should take the risk and
reap the pleasure from this soup.

> 500 g tripe
> 1 onion, finely chopped
> 1 dessertspoon sage, finely chopped
> 1 dessertspoon rosemary, finely chopped
> 1 bay leaf, crumbled
> 300 g tomatoes, peeled and deseeded if fresh, or
>   sieved if tinned
> 50 ml olive oil
> 500 ml broth (pp.46-8)
> salt
> pepper
> *Parmigiano* cheese, freshly grated
> 1 generous slice per person of day old bread, toasted
>   if preferred

Sauté the onion in a cooking pot, then add the tripe, cut in
ribbons, with the sage, bay leaf and rosemary. Cook for a few
minutes, add salt and pepper to taste, then cover and cook
over a reduced heat for about fifteen minutes. It is better if
the tripe cooks in its own juices, but if it dries out a little, add
some water. After fifteen minutes add the tomatoes and
broth; cover and cook for a further five minutes. Put the
slices of bread in serving plates, ladle the tripe soup over
them and sprinkle generously with *Parmigiano* cheese.

Stracciatella

Torn eggs

The name of this popular Roman soup literally means torn eggs. It is simple to make and quite delicious and sustaining — you can almost 'feel it doing you good!' This version is only one of many — you will find similar recipes in almost every type of cuisine with perhaps the best-known varieties being from Greek and Chinese kitchens.

> 3 litres chicken broth (p.48)
> 4 eggs
> 4 dessertspoons *semolina*
> a little nutmeg, freshly grated
> black pepper, freshly ground
> *Parmigiano* cheese, freshly grated
> extra *Parmigiano* cheese, freshly grated

Bring the chicken broth to the boil. Meanwhile, mix thoroughly all the remaining ingredients. Once the broth is ready (it is important that it is boiling and not just hot) pour the egg mixture in a thin stream into the broth stirring slowly as you do so with a large fork in a back and forth movement. Do not whisk the eggs in as you will mix them completely with the broth. The broth cooks the egg mixture, keeping it in strands — the torn eggs of the soup's name.

Serve immediately with extra *Parmigiano* cheese if desired.

Zuppa delle quattro stagioni

Soup of the four seasons

This is a versatile soup, as its name indicates. Without changing the method of preparation it can be eaten hot on a winter's day or cold in the summer.

> 150 g fresh *borlotti* (red) beans, shelled (tinned beans can be used if necessary)
> ½ cabbage, finely chopped
> 100 g spinach, washed thoroughly and coarsely chopped
> 3 medium-sized potatoes, peeled and cubed
> a few fresh French beans, chopped
> 500 g fresh peas, shelled
> 2 small onions, finely chopped
> 1 stalk celery, finely chopped
> 2 cloves garlic, finely chopped
> 2 tablespoons parsley, finely chopped
> 75 ml olive oil
> 2½ litres water
> salt
> short pasta (p.46)
> *Parmigiano* cheese, freshly grated

Boil the water in a very large soup pot. Add all the other ingredients including the oil and gently boil, covered for one hour. Add the pasta, stir and cook until *al dente*. Serve with plenty of *Parmigiano* cheese.

Pasta e ceci alla Romana

Chick pea soup — Roman style

This is a delicious soup from the Rome region. It is economical and quick to make and the rosemary and anchovies fill the kitchen with a wonderful aroma as they cook, indicating the tastes to follow.

> 400 g chick peas (dried or tinned)
> 2 cloves garlic
> 2 sprigs rosemary, finely chopped
> ½ hot red chilli, finely chopped
> 3 anchovy fillets, finely chopped
> 75 ml oil
> 1½ litres water
> short pasta (p.46)

If you are using dried chick peas, soak them in salted water overnight before use; if you are using the tinned variety, drain and rinse them well before proceeding.

Crush one clove of garlic to a smooth paste and add the chopped rosemary, chopped chilli and anchovy fillets. Pound these ingredients together to form a paste. Heat the oil and fry the garlic mixture and the chick peas over high heat for two to three minutes. Add the water, cover and cook slowly for forty-five minutes.

When you are ready to serve the soup bring it to the boil, add some short pasta and cook until *al dente*. Serve immediately.

Zuppa di spinaci

Spinach soup

This is another soup served over stale bread, but as in the other recipes short pasta may be used instead just as successfully. You may replace the spinach with silver beet but in this case trim it very carefully to remove all trace of the coarse white fibres.

> 50 g butter
> 1 bunch spinach, thoroughly washed and coarsely
> cut
> 1½ litres broth (pp.46-8)
> ½ litre milk
> a little nutmeg, freshly grated
> *Parmigiano* cheese, freshly grated
> 1 slice of lightly toasted or stale bread per person

Melt the butter in a large pot, add the spinach and cook it until the water given off by the spinach has evaporated. Add the broth and boil gently for five minutes. Incorporate the milk, nutmeg, and 2 tablespoons of *Parmigiano* cheese. Place a slice of lightly toasted or fried stale bread in individual soup bowls and gently ladle the soup over them. Serve with additional *Parmigiano* cheese.

Zuppa di broccoli

Broccoli soup

This vegetable soup is based on a Roman recipe and the strong green colour that the broccoli imparts was always regarded by the Romans as aesthetically pleasing. Modern tastes still comply with that feeling, assisted of course by the delicious flavour of the broccoli. If broccoli is unavailable, an equally delicious soup, although not as exciting visually, can be made from cauliflower.

1 kg broccoli
75 ml olive oil
2 cloves garlic, crushed
1 dessertspoon parsley, chopped
3 litres water
salt
black pepper, freshly ground
500 g short pasta (p.46)
pecorino cheese, freshly grated

Wash and trim the broccoli (or cauliflower if used) of all tough stalks and outer leaves before breaking it into small flowerettes. Heat the oil in a large soup pot and lightly brown the garlic. Add the parsley. Pour in the water with salt and pepper to taste and bring to the boil. Add the broccoli and short pasta and boil until *al dente*. Add abundant quantities of *pecorino* cheese to the soup, stir and remove from the heat. Serve with extra *pecorino* if desired.

Zuppa acquacotta

Soup of cooked water

Despite its unpromising name this soup is delicious and sustaining.
Using Australian field mushrooms you will achieve a much darker
soup than that achieved by the white Italian mushrooms. This does
not, however, detract at all from the flavour.

> 75 ml olive oil
> 1 clove garlic, finely chopped
> 350 g mushrooms, wiped free of any soil, not
>   washed, and finely sliced
> 150 g tomatoes, skinned and deseeded if fresh, or
>   sieved if tinned
> salt
> 2 litres water
> 1 slice toasted stale bread per person
> 2 eggs
> *Parmigiano* cheese, freshly grated

Heat the oil in a large pot, add the garlic and fry gently to a
golden brown. Add the mushrooms and cook for about two
minutes or until they settle. Then add the tomatoes plus half
their quantity in water and an additional 2 litres of salted
water. Bring to the boil, cover and cook slowly for forty-five
minutes. Place a piece of toasted bread in the bottom of
individual pre-heated serving bowls. Bring the soup to
boiling point and remove from the heat. Beat the eggs well
and pour into the hot soup stirring continuously. Ladle the
soup over the bread and serve with the *Parmigiano* cheese.

Zuppa di cipolline

Soup of tiny white onions

Use the smallest white onions you can find for this soup. If they are not available you can slice large ones but the taste will not be as good nor as sweet as that provided by the small onions.

> 100 ml olive oil
> 600 g tiny white onions, peeled and left whole
> water
> salt
> black pepper, freshly grated
> 2 tomatoes peeled, deseeded and chopped if fresh, 4
>   tomatoes sieved if tinned
> *spaghettini* (p.46)
> *Parmigiano* cheese, freshly grated

Heat the oil in a large soup pot and very lightly brown the onions. Add water to cover, salt and pepper and the tomatoes. Cover the pot and simmer gently until the onions have softened. Bring the soup to the boil and add the *spaghettini*, which you have broken into short pieces, to the pot. Cook until *al dente*. This soup should not be allowed to become too watery; if this does happen boil it hard with the lid off to reduce the amount of liquid. Serve the soup hot with plenty of *Parmigiano* cheese.

Cipollata Toscana

Onion soup

As its name suggests, this soup originated in the Tuscany region of Italy. Legend has it that the **cipollata** is the forerunner of the familiar French onion soup and that it was brought to France in the 1530s when Catherine de Medici married King Henry II. The soup is served traditionally with bread although pasta can be substituted.

> 1½ litres water
> 3 large onions, thickly sliced
> 500 g tomatoes, peeled and deseeded if fresh, or
>   sieved if tinned
> 3 tablespoons fresh parsley, chopped
> salt
> black pepper, freshly ground
> 100 ml olive oil
> 1 slice of stale brown bread per person
> generous pinch dried oregano

Bring the water to boil and add to it the onions, tomatoes, parsley, salt, pepper and oil. Cook, covered, over low heat until the onion is soft. Place a slice of bread in individual soup bowls. Sprinkle each slice with a little oregano and gently ladle the *cippollata* over them. Serve very hot.

Minestra di fagioli e baccala

Bean and stockfish soup

This old and much prized Venetian dish is one of the first recipes to be recorded in early Italian cookbooks. Like many dishes of the sixteenth century, it is strongly flavoured.

> 300 g baccala (stockfish), which can be obtained
>   from markets and continental grocers, ready
>   to cook
> 500 g borlotti beans, fresh if possible, otherwise dry
>   beans should be soaked overnight
> 300 g tomatoes, peeled and deseeded if fresh, or
>   sieved if tinned
> 3 cloves garlic, one clove finely chopped
> 2 tablespoons parsley, finely chopped
> 2 small, hot red peppers
> 50 ml olive oil
> salt
> black pepper, freshly ground
> 300 g short pasta

Cover the beans with water, add a little salt, some pepper and two whole cloves of garlic. Cook for about forty minutes. At this time take out the garlic, add the baccala (which should be cut into large chunks), tomatoes, small red peppers, finely chopped garlic and parsley. If necessary add more hot water before cooking for a further ten minutes. Add the pasta and when cooked pour over the olive oil and sprinkle with some more black pepper.

Casareccia

Fish soup

This superb fish soup requires care in the preparation but the
results are richly rewarding. When selecting the kilogram of mixed
fish, we suggest you see what is the bargain in the market. It can
even include heads and bones which the fishmonger is discarding.
Just ensure you choose flavoursome fish such as red mullet,
schnapper, sand whiting, gurnet. Also, remember the broth should
be strained at least twice to remove fat.

> 3 litres water
> 1 celery stalk with leaves, cut in 3
> 1 bay leaf
> 200 ml olive oil
> 1 gurnet fish, including skin and bones, in large
>   chunks
> 1 kg mixed fish
> 1 glass white wine
> 1 dessertspoon of salt (optional)
> 3 cloves garlic, finely chopped
> 500 g *calamaretti* (small squid) peeled, washed and
>   cut into rings
> 2 anchovy fillets
> 500 g tomatoes, deeseded and chopped if fresh,
>   sieved if tinned
> 1 teaspoon black pepper, freshly ground
> 2 dessertspoons parsley, finely chopped
> 1 kg mussels, well washed
> 1 kg clams, well washed
> day-old bread, sliced and oven toasted

Have three cooking pots at your disposal.

In the first pot, which is best placed on the back burner
of the stove, combine the water, celery, bay leaf, half the oil,
gurnet, mixed fish, white wine and salt. Bring to the boil and
cook at a fast boil for fifteen minutes, reduce the heat and
simmer another fifteen minutes. Remove from the heat,

strain through fine muslin, and allow to cool. Skin, bone and break into small pieces the gurnet and other fish and set aside.

In the second pot, lightly fry the garlic in the remaining oil. When the garlic is golden, add the squid and anchovy fillets, tomatoes, pepper and parsley. Cook for fifteen minutes and set aside.

In the third pot steam open the mussels and clams. Remove from the heat. Remove the flesh from the shells, cutting the large mussels in half, and set aside. Strain the pan juices to eliminate any sediment.

Strain again the cooled fish broth from the first pot. Combine with the boned and skinned fish pieces, the shell fish and their juices. Simmer for thirty minutes. Place a piece of bread in individual bowls and ladle this delicious fish soup over each.

Semolina in brodo

Semolina with broth

This is one of the oldest traditional soups from Lazio. It is economical and quick to make and very tasty.

2 ½ litres beef broth (p.47)
150 g *semolina*
Parmigiano cheese, freshly grated

Bring the broth to boiling point and slowly sieve the *semolina* into it, stirring frequently to prevent lumps forming. Cook covered over a low flame for about ten minutes. Serve hot and with generous servings of *Parmigiano* cheese.

Gnocchetti in brodo

Gnocchetti in broth

These **gnocchetti** are flavoured with minced chicken but there is no limit to the flavouring you may use. Experiment with mixtures of **proscuitto** or **mortadella** and chicken, finely minced lean pork or veal or combinations of meats and spices left over from other dishes.

> 2 chicken breasts, skinned and beaten flat
> 50 g butter
> 4 eggs
> salt
> black pepper, freshly ground
> ½ a nutmeg, freshly grated
> 500 g flour
> 3 litres beef and chicken broth (p.47)
> *Parmigiano* cheese, freshly grated

Poach the chicken breasts gently in water until they are tender. Drain them well and mince them very finely in a food processor or blender. Melt the butter in a small saucepan, allow it to cool a little and then beat in the eggs, salt, pepper and nutmeg.

Add the egg and butter mixture to the minced chicken and the flour and combine thoroughly.

Turn the mixture on to a floured board and knead with the heel of your hand for five minutes. The dough should be soft to the touch. Cut the dough into four equal portions and cover three of them with an inverted plate or bowl. Flour the board and your hands again and roll the fourth piece of dough with the flat of your hand and fingers into a long thin sausage shape ½ to 1 centimetre in diameter and about 35 centimetres in length. Cut into ½-centimetre nuggets. Repeat the process with each of the other three pieces of dough.

Bring the broth to boiling point and gently add the *gnocchetti*. Cook at a gentle simmer for ten to twelve minutes and serve in the broth accompanied by abundant quantities of *Parmigiano* cheese.

Gnocchetti di spinaci in brodo

Spinach gnocchetti in broth

Spinach **gnocchetti** *are delicious dark green dumplings. They are smaller than* **gnocchi** *and although you can serve them with cream sauces such as* **crema alla Gorgonzola** *(p.128) they are at their* very best cooked and served **in brodo.**

> 150 g cooked spinach (make sure that you have
>   thoroughly washed the spinach before cooking
>   in a little buter)
> 50 g crustless brown bread
> milk
> ½ teaspoon salt
> ½ a nutmeg, freshly grated
> 1 egg yolk
> 1 tablespoon cream
> 15 g *Parmigiano* cheese, freshly grated
> 3 litres beef and chicken broth (p.47)
> flour
> extra *Parmigiano* cheese, freshly grated

Remove any excess moisture in the cooked spinach by gently squeezing it in your hands and then patting it dry in a clean tea towel. Put the spinach into a bowl with the bread which has been moistened with a very little (1 tablespoon at the most) milk. Add the salt, nutmeg, the egg yolk, cream and *Parmigiano* cheese. Mix these ingredients together until they are well combined.

Flour a working board and your hands well, turn the mixture out on to the board and knead with the heel of your hand for five minutes. Cut the dough into four equal portions and cover three of these with an inverted plate or bowl. Flour the board and your hands again and roll the fourth piece of dough with the flat of your hand and fingers into a long thin sausage shape ½ to 1 centimetre in diameter and about 35 centimetres in length. Cut into ½-centimetre nuggets. Repeat the process with each of the other three pieces of dough.

Bring the broth to boiling point and gently add the *gnocchetti*. When the broth returns to the boil the *gnocchetti* are ready. Serve very hot in the broth and with a generous amount of the extra *Parmigiano* cheese.

RISOTTO

Rice dishes

Rice was introduced into Europe from India and China two thousand years ago and came to Italy via Greece and Portugal. Rice-based dishes — risotto — are a staple part of *cucina Italiana* and here we offer a brief selection of some of the tastiest of them, drawn from several of the regions of Italy.

Risotto al chianti

Rice with chianti

This mixture of rice and wine is a rare recipe from Tuscany. You will find their combination to be a unique experience.

400 g rice
2 tablespoons butter
½ onion, finely chopped
½ stick of celery, finely chopped
1 carrot, finely chopped
½ bottle *chianti*
500 ml broth (pp.46-8)
4 tablespoons *Parmigiano* cheese, freshly grated
salt
pepper

Chop the celery, onion and carrot finely. Sauté in the cooking pot with half the butter, over a low heat, for about ten minutes. Add the rice and stir for a couple of minutes. Pour in the broth and the *chianti*. Bring to the boil and cook for another 10-12 minutes. Remove pot from the heat, add the *Parmigiano* cheese, the rest of the butter, salt and pepper to taste. Let it rest for a couple of minutes and then serve.

Riso e fave

Rice with broad beans

This dish originated in Lazio. As with most Italian recipes, there are many regional variations. The one printed here is particularly appreciated in Rome.

> 400 g rice
> 250 g broad beans, shelled
> 70 g *prosciutto* ham, finely chopped
> 70 g butter
> 70 g *Parmigiano* cheese, freshly grated
> 1 dessertspoon parsley, finely chopped
> 1 clove garlic, finely chopped
> 1 litre broth (pp.46-8)
> salt
> pepper

Have the simmering broth at the ready. Lightly brown the ham, garlic and parsley. Stir in a ladle of broth. When this starts to boil, add a pinch of salt and the rice. Stirring frequently, pour in more broth as the rice absorbs the liquid and continue until the rice is nearly cooked. In the meantime boil the broad beans for ten minutes. Then skin them. A few minutes before the rice is ready, add the skinned broad beans. Cook for a few more minutes. Sprinkle generously with *Parmigiano* cheese and white pepper.

Risotto ai porri

Rice with leeks

This is a medieval recipe from Tuscany, which seems to have originated in a monastery in Florence. The result is still a surprising and excellent dish.

> 350 g rice
> 300 ml cream
> 100 g butter
> 50 g bacon, finely chopped
> 20 g flour
> 6 medium sized leeks, washed and finely chopped
> 1 small onion, finely chopped
> 1 chicken stock cube
> 2 eggs
> ½ glass dry white wine
> 1 litre broth (pp.46-8)
> 5 tablespoons *Parmigiano* cheese, freshly grated

Cut up the bacon and onion and put them in the pot in which you intend to make the *risotto*. Wash the leeks and cut them finely. Add them to the bacon and onion and sauté together with half the butter over a gentle heat until half cooked. If necessary, add a few spoonsful of broth. Add the rice and stir. Pour in the wine and gently stir again until the wine has evaporated. Mix in a ladle of boiling broth. As the rice absorbs the broth add more and continue until it is cooked. About ten minutes before the rice is done, heat the rest of the butter in a small pan. Add flour and cook until the consistency is smooth. Pour in the cream and half a crumbled chicken stock cube. Stir continuously until it comes to the boil. Remove from the heat and add one tablespoon of grated *Parmigiano* cheese and — one at a time — the yolks of two eggs. Pour this mixture into the cooked rice. Add extra butter and *Parmigiano*. Mix well and serve.

Riso allo yoghurt

Rice with yoghurt

This fine, light vegetarian dish seems to have been introduced into Italy from Turkey.

400 g natural yoghurt
400 g rice
1 tablespoon butter
1 onion, finely chopped
1 tablespoon parsley, finely chopped
1 teaspoon paprika
1 litre broth (pp.46-8)

Chop the onion finely and sauté it in the butter. Add rice. Bring the broth to the boil. Stir the rice and onion over a moderate heat for a few minutes and then tip them into the boiling broth. Reduce heat and simmer, covered, for 15 minutes. Ladle the soup into serving plates, top with yoghurt, sprinkle with paprika and parsley and serve hot.

Risotto con zucca

Rice with pumpkin

This is a simple, light springtime dish, enjoyed in the lower part of Lombardy. There the best known restaurants consider that they serve some of the finest rice dishes in all Italy.

> 400 g rice
> 500 g good quality yellow pumpkin
> 2 tablespoons butter
> 4 tablespoons *Parmigiano* cheese, freshly grated
> 2 chicken stock cubes
> salt

Peel the pumpkin and cut it into small cubes. Put them in the pot and cook with half the butter, and a small quantity of water, until the pumpkin has begun to soften. Add rice and stir. Cook for a few moments before adding more boiling water and the two crumbled chicken stock cubes. Stir the sauce continually, adding more boiling water from time to time, until the rice is cooked. Add the rest of the butter and the *Parmigiano* cheese, as well as salt if required, and serve hot.

PASTA ASCIUTTA

'Dry' pasta served with sauces

Pasta asciutta is traditionally eaten as a first course, although it is popular to eat it in Australia as a complete meal in itself or sometimes as a second course. Its place in the meal will therefore determine how much pasta you need to cook.

These recipes, unless otherwise stated, will serve six people. Allow 75-100 grams of pasta per head for a first course and 100-150 grams for a more substantial serving.

Salsa di pomodoro
Tomato sauce

Salsa di pomodoro *is the principal sauce in all kinds of Italian cooking. It is also by far the most popular as well as one of the simplest sauces to accompany pasta. Only five recipes are given here, when in fact almost a whole book could be devoted to the numerous recipes based on this extraordinary fruit. We hope to guide you only, so that you can enjoy many and varied tomato sauce recipes based on your own improvisation.*

The demise of the tomato along with many other fruits and vegetables is well known and written about at length in most cookery books. Unless you are able to grow your own plants and harvest as the fruit ripens or purchase tomatoes from a rare, scrupulous and astute greengrocer it is most unlikely that you will be able to produce a good tomato sauce. There is little or no point in using chalky and insipid tomatoes for which you have all too often paid a king's ransom — the resulting sauce will similarly be insipid and unfortunately worthless. When good ripe fresh tomatoes are not available it is much better to use tinned plum tomatoes, preferably the imported Italian variety.

> 75 ml olive oil
> 2 cloves garlic
> 30 g onion, finely sliced
> 500 g of tomatoes, peeled and deseeded if fresh,
>   or sieved if tinned
> salt
> black pepper, freshly ground
> 45-50 g butter
> pasta (see above)

84

Peel the garlic and with a small sharp knife snick out the two 'eyes' from each end of the clove. Insert two toothpicks diagonally through each clove. This will enable you to find and retrieve the garlic at the end of cooking time.

Heat the oil in a saucepan, add the garlic and onion, and fry gently until the onion browns evenly. Do not allow the mixture to burn. Add the tomatoes and leave the sauce over a moderate heat stirring from time to time. This will take twenty-five to thirty minutes. Add salt and black pepper to taste and swirl in the knob of butter. Remove and discard the garlic.

When this sauce is cooked you will have virtually a smooth red sauce, the onions will have almost completely melted away and the bottom of the saucepan will be quite clean, as this sauce does not stick.

Serve with any pasta of your choice.

Sugo svelto
Quick sauce

*This tomato-based sauce, true to its name, should only take fifteen minutes from the time of deciding to make it to serving. For some reason this sauce acquired an alternative and colourful nickname — **sugo alla puttanesca** — 'the prostitutes' sauce'.*

50 g butter
75 ml olive oil
2 cloves garlic, finely chopped
6 anchovy fillets, chopped
200 g black olives, pitted and chopped
1 dessertspoon capers, chopped
500 g tomatoes, peeled and deseeded if fresh, or
    sieved if tinned
1 dessertspoon parsley, chopped
black pepper, freshly ground
pasta (p.84)

Heat the butter and oil in a saucepan taking care to not burn the butter. Add the garlic and anchovies and fry over moderate heat until the garlic turns golden. Add the olives, capers, tomatoes and parsley. Cook over a high flame for three to five minutes, shaking the pan from time to time to avoid catching. Add black pepper to taste and serve immediately with the pasta of your choice.

Salsa di pomodoro al limone

Tomato and lemon sauce

This is a particularly light and refreshing sauce and ideal for summer outdoor eating. Even the current fashion for cold pasta dishes is understandable when you try this sauce. Fresh basil brings out the full flavours of the ingredients, but the dried herb can be used if you have no alternative.

> 100 ml olive oil
> 150 g fresh basil (or 1 tablespoon dried basil)
> strained juice of half a lemon
> 500 g tomatoes, peeled and deseeded if fresh, or
>   sieved if tinned
> black pepper, freshly ground
> pasta (p.84)

Heat the olive oil over high heat, add the remainder of the ingredients in the order in which they are listed at one-minute intervals. Moderate the heat and cook for ten minutes, stirring the sauce occasionally.

If you choose to use this sauce cold, cook the pasta in the usual way. When it is *al dente* add a tumbler of iced water to the pot and drain immediately. Cool the pasta under running cold water. Drain thoroughly and toss the pasta in cold *salsa di pomodoro al limone*, chill until ready to serve. Never serve cheese with cold pasta.

Salsa di basilico
Tomato and basil sauce

This is another version of the basic tomato sauce on pp.84-5. Try to use fresh basil only. The dried herb can be used if you have no alternative, but it is a quite different flavour and not as good. The varieties of tomato sauce are numerous and you can also adapt and improvise on the traditional versions yourself. All fresh herbs make a wonderful marriage with tomatoes (although the combination with basil is probably the finest) and they can be added individually or in combinations and to a greater or lesser degree as your taste and the rest of your menu decree.

75 ml olive oil
30 g onion, finely sliced
2 cloves garlic
500 g tomatoes, peeled and deseeded if fresh, or
    sieved if tinned
1 handful fresh basil, chopped
pasta (p.84)

Peel and prepare the garlic as for *salsa di pomodoro*. Heat the oil in a saucepan, add the onion and garlic and fry over moderate heat until the onion is evenly browned. Do not allow the mixture to burn. Add the tomatoes and basil, bring the sauce to the boil then reduce the heat and gently simmer uncovered for half an hour. Serve with any pasta of your choice.

Spaghetti del marinaio
Sailors' spaghetti

The true **spaghetti del marinaio** or **spaghetti marinara**
contains no seafood: it is in fact another variety of tomato sauce.
One explanation for this deceptive name is that traditionally sailors
hate eating fish. Whatever the reason it is a very good sauce.

> 150 ml olive oil
> 3 cloves garlic, finely chopped
> 1 small hot red chilli, deseeded and chopped
> 500 g tomatoes, peeled and deseeded if fresh, or
>   sieved if tinned
> 2 sprigs of fresh basil, finely chopped
> salt
> black pepper, freshly ground
> *Parmigiano* cheese, freshly grated
> pasta (p.84)

Heat the oil in a saucepan over a high flame. Add the garlic
and chilli. As soon as the garlic is golden add the tomatoes,
basil and salt to taste. Reduce the heat to medium and cook,
stirring occasionally, for eight to ten minutes. Serve with
spaghetti and plenty of *Parmigiano* cheese.

Salsa con acciughe e pomodoro

Anchovy and tomato sauce

This is another variation of the standard tomato sauce (pp. 84-5).
It is quick and easy to prepare and is best served with **fusilli**.

> 75 ml oil (including the oil from the anchovies)
> 2 cloves garlic, crushed
> 1 kg tomatoes, peeled and deseeded if fresh, or sieved
>   if tinned
> 1 tin anchovy fillets, chopped
> black pepper, freshly ground
> pasta (p.84)

Heat the oil and lightly brown the garlic. Add all the other
ingredients, mix well and cook over moderate heat for five
minutes, stirring occasionally. Toss gently with the pasta of
your choice and serve at once.

Fusilli alla panna e prosciutto

Fusilli with cream and ham

For this dish you can use either **prosciutto** or cooked ham. The
success of this simple sauce lies in adding the **Parmigiano** cheese
at the right time and mixing it in properly.

> 100 g ham, sliced finely
> 50 g butter
> 50 g Parmigiano cheese, freshly grated
> 100 ml cream
> salt
> 400 g fusilli

Cook the fusilli until it is al dente, then strain. Melt half the
butter in a large pan, add the strips of ham and sauté for a few
moments. Toss in the drained fusilli, pour cream over it and
mix well. Remove from the heat, add the rest of the butter
and the grated Parmigiano. Mix again and serve.

Salsa all'aglio e olio

Garlic and oil sauce

This is a wonderful sauce to make. It fills the kitchen with a mouth-watering aroma and is a delight for all garlic lovers. The dish is quick to prepare but can be quite a test for the inexperienced cook as the sauce will burn very quickly if you do not take care. It is important to use good quality olive oil for this sauce and to make sure that the garlic is very fresh.

> 100 ml olive oil
> 5 cloves garlic, finely chopped
> black pepper, freshly ground
> 2-3 tablespoons water
> 1 tablespoon parsley, finely chopped
> *Parmigiano* cheese, freshly grated
> pasta (p.84)

Heat the oil in a saucepan over high heat, add the garlic and pepper and cook carefully until the garlic is golden. Add the water and the parsley and allow the water to evaporate, taking care that the oil and garlic do not burn and that the parsley does not lose its bright green colour. Toss some already cooked *spaghetti* with the sauce and serve immediately with plenty of *Parmigiano* cheese. Have a peppermill to hand.

Pesto alla Genovese

Basil sauce

Gourmets and gluttons alike wax lyrical over the joys of **pesto**. Its
name is redolent of summer and the Italian Riviera. It is delicious
with **gnocchi** or **tagliatelle** or for that matter any pasta, and is
wonderful stirred into individual bowls of almost all soups.

Pesto cannot be made with dried basil; you must therefore
make the most of the summer supply. In Australian conditions
basil is easy to grow and it is wonderful to have a few pots of it
either on the window-sill or close by the kitchen door. Bunches of
fresh basil are also becoming increasingly available at all good
greengrocers and at fruit and vegetable markets.

Pesto is traditionally made in a marble mortar with a
hardwood pestle, and purists would claim that this is indeed the
only way it can be made. The food processor or blender, however,
does a more than adequate job and, although the **pesto** may not be
as rich, smooth and as aromatic as that made with a mortar and
pestle, the **pesto** it produces is still very good. **Pesto** freezes well,
as does the fresh herb if you interlay sheets of freezer paper
between branches of freshly picked basil; and although not quite as
delicious as freshly made **pesto**, it is certainly not to be ignored.

1 large bunch fresh basil
½ cup pine nuts
5 cloves garlic
2 tablespoons *pecorino* cheese, freshly grated
2 tablespoons *Parmigiano* cheese, freshly grated
salt
150 ml olive oil
pasta (p.84)

Pesto 1 — by mortar and pestle

Remove any stems or blemishes from the basil leaves. In a large mortar put the basil, garlic, pine nuts and salt and, using a rotary action, crush all the ingredients to a paste with the pestle. Add both the cheeses, and continue to blend the ingredients until the cheeses are completely incorporated into the paste. Now add the oil drop by drop at first and then in a very slow stream, making sure that all the oil is being completely amalgamated with the basil paste as you go. Serve with pasta of your choice and a little extra butter.

Pesto 2 — by food processor

Remove any stems or blemishes from the basil leaves. Place all the ingredients except the oil in the bowl of the food processor and purée to a paste, making sure to scrape down the sides of the bowl. As the processor is working pour in oil in a slow stream. Continue to purée until you have a smooth paste and all of the oil is amalgamated with the other ingredients. Serve with pasta of your choice and a little extra butter.

Pasta alla salvia

Sage sauce

Like the **pesto alla Genovese** on p.92, this sauce can only be made with the fresh herb. It does not freeze well so it is best to make the most of it when you have plenty of sage in the garden. Sage is quite hardy and grows quickly and well in Australian conditions. An absorbent pasta such as **tagliatelle** or **gnocchi** is best suited to this sauce.

> 150 ml olive oil
> 50 g butter
> 2 cloves garlic, finely chopped
> 6 sprigs fresh sage, finely chopped
> salt
> black pepper, freshly ground
> *Parmigiano* cheese, freshly grated (optional)
> pasta (p.84)

Heat the oil and butter in a saucepan, add the garlic and cook until it is golden brown, taking care that the butter does not burn. Add the sage leaves, salt and pepper and cook for only a minute to release the full flavour and aroma of the sage. Add the already cooked pasta to the saucepan, toss the sauce through it gently and serve immediately, accompanied by *Parmigiano* cheese if required.

Pasta con salvia

Pasta with sage sauce

This is a dish typical of Emilia-Romagna; and is another and more complex use of the herb sage. With a change of herb, sauces characteristic of other regions are created.

> 200 g veal, minced
> 50 g *prosciutto*, finely chopped
> 1 small onion, finely chopped
> 1 small carrot, finely chopped
> 1 dessertspoon parsley, finely chopped
> ½ glass dry white wine
> 5 sprigs fresh sage
> 50 ml olive oil
> *Parmigiano* cheese, freshly grated
> salt
> pepper
> 500 g short pasta, for instance *macaroni* or *penne*
> 200 ml broth (pp.46-8)

Lightly fry the veal, ham, onion, carrot and parsley in oil. When the mixture is golden add the wine and after this has evaporated, add salt and pepper, sage leaves and the broth. Then let the sauce cook slowly for about an hour, adding a little more broth when necessary. Cook the pasta until *al dente*, strain, mix with the sauce. The sage leaves should be removed at this point. Top the sauce with a good dusting of *Parmigiano* cheese.

Maccheroni alla maggiorana

Macaroni with marjoram

This is a sauce which originated in Calabria, though it is now made in all parts of Italy. Its taste will vary according to the use of sausages which are peculiar to the various regions.

> 500 g tomatoes, peeled and deseeded if fresh, or sieved if tinned
> 100 g continental sausages, finely chopped and skinned
> 80 g *Parmigiano* cheese, freshly grated
> 50 g butter
> 1 small onion, finely chopped
> 1 carrot, finely chopped
> 1 bay leaf
> 1 dessertspoon marjoram
> a little broth (pp.46-8)
> salt
> pepper
> 400 g *macaroni*

Sauté the finely chopped onion and carrot in butter with the bay leaf. Skin and cut up the sausages and add them to the cooking pot. Mix them well with the other ingredients, then cook until the sausage begins to brown. Add tomatoes and a little broth, together with salt and pepper to taste. Stir until the sauce thickens. Remove from the heat and add the marjoram. Cook the *marcaroni* in boiling, salted water until it is *al dente*. Mix with the sauce and serve topped with grated *Parmigiano* cheese.

Spaghetti alla Siciliana
Sicilian spaghetti

Anchovy and oregano strongly flavour a sauce which is very easy to make.

100 ml olive oil
2 cloves garlic, finely chopped
black pepper, freshly ground
6 anchovy fillets, chopped
15 g capers
18 green olives, pitted and roughly chopped
500 g tomatoes, peeled and deseeded if fresh, or
   sieved if tinned
1 tablespoon parsley, finely chopped
2 sprigs basil, finely chopped
1 sprig oregano, finely chopped (or 1 teaspoon dried
   oregano)
pasta (p.84)

Heat the oil in a saucepan and gently fry the garlic and a little black pepper until the garlic is golden. Add the remaining ingredients. Bring to the boil then reduce the heat and cook, covered, over a low flame for twenty minutes. Serve hot with *spaghetti*.

Penne alla Vesuviana
Penne Vesuvius style

This is a typical Neapolitan dish, named because it was first enjoyed in the shadow of Mount Vesuvius.

> 1 kg tomatoes, peeled and deseeded if fresh, or sieved if tinned
> 800 g yearling beef
> 50 g *prosciutto crudo* (cured raw ham)
> 1 tablespoon sultanas
> 1 tablespoon pine nuts
> 50 g *pancetta*
> 2 cloves garlic, sliced
> 1 tablespoon parsley, finely chopped
> ½ onion, finely chopped
> 1 glass white wine
> 4 tablespoons *pecorino* cheese, freshly grated
> 50 ml olive oil
> salt
> pepper
> 500 g *penne*

Cut up all the *prosciutto* and half the *pancetta*. Put the sultanas to soak in water. Slice the garlic. Make incisions in the beef and place in them pieces of *prosciutto*, *pancetta*, garlic, parsley, sultanas and pine nuts. Rub the meat with salt and pepper and cook it in a pot with oil and the remaining *pancetta* and onion. Lightly brown the beef on all sides. Pour the wine over it and cook until the wine has evaporated. Add tomatoes, salt and pepper to taste and two glasses of water. Cover and cook gently for three hours. Add extra water from time to time if necessary. When the meat is ready, cook the *penne* in boiling salted water until *al dente*. Remove the meat from the sauce, slice it and put it aside. Strain the *penne*, mix it with the sauce and sprinkle the *pecorino* cheese over it. Top with slices of meat and serve.

Ragu Buono
'The Good Sauce'

In Italy this marvellous sauce is traditionally made for the main Sunday meal. It is best eaten with **pasta all'uovo** — that is, one made from eggs, such as **tagliatelle**.

> 300 g lean meat, minced or cut into small cubes — a
>   mixture of veal and pork is best for this
> 500 g tomatoes, peeled and deseeded if fresh, or
>   sieved if tinned
> 1 onion, finely chopped
> 1 carrot, finely chopped
> a few basil leaves
> 1 stick of celery, chopped
> 75 ml olive oil
> salt
> black pepper, freshly ground
> pasta (p.84)

Put the onion, carrot and celery into a pot with the olive oil. Brown them together lightly, before adding the meat which should be stirred and then left to cook for a few minutes. Now add the tomatoes, basil, salt and pepper. Cook over a moderate heat for one and a half hours.

Maccheroni Casinalbo

Macaroni Casinalbo

This delicious sauce is named after a small town in the Emilia-Romagna region, near Modena.

400 g eggplant, peeled and cut into cubes
300 g tomatoes, peeled and deseeded if fresh, or
sieved if tinned
150 g beef, cut into small cubes
100 g butter
80 g *Parmigiano* cheese, freshly grated
1 clove garlic, crushed
1 small onion, finely sliced
salt
pepper
a little flour
300 g *maccheroni*

Sauté the onion and crushed garlic in 50 g of butter till
golden, then remove the garlic. Add the beef and brown
over a high heat. Add the tomatoes, pepper and salt; reduce
the heat and let simmer for about thirty minutes. Peel the
eggplants; cut them in cubes which should then be lightly
covered in flour. Fry them until golden in the remaining
butter. Remove them from the pan and place them on
absorbent paper to dry before adding them to the meat sauce.
Cook the macaroni in salted water until *al dente*. Strain and
mix it with the eggplant sauce. Cover with grated *Parmigiano*
cheese.

Penne alla Calabrese
Penne Calabrese style

This dish is a touch hot, which is one indication of its Calabrian origin.

> 150 g hot salami (*piccante*), diced
> 500 g tomatoes, peeled and deseeded if fresh, or
> sieved if tinned
> 2 hardboiled eggs, sliced
> 500 g green olives, pitted
> 50 g black olives, pitted
> oregano
> salt
> pepper
> 50 ml olive oil
> 400 g *penne*

Cook the tomatoes in oil lightly for about thirty minutes, then add the olives and oregano, salt and pepper to taste. Simmer for another ten minutes. Cook the *penne* in salted water and strain while it is still very firm to the bite. Mix the pasta with the sauce. Butter an ovenproof casserole. Put the pasta in it and cover with the diced salami, sliced hardboiled eggs, then cook in a pre-heated oven for ten minutes.

Spaghetti alla Perugina
Spaghetti Perugia style

This delightful recipe originated in the Umbrian region.

> 250 ml *besciamella* sauce (p.127)
> 2 continental sausages or 100 g salami, finely
>   chopped
> 1 white onion, finely chopped
> 50 g butter
> salt
> pepper
> 400 g *spaghetti*

Finely chop the onion and sauté it in the butter until golden.
Add the skinned and chopped sausages or the salami,
chopped small. Cook for a few minutes, then mix in the
besciamella sauce. Let simmer for another ten minutes over a
low heat. In the meantime cook the spaghetti until it is *al
dente*, strain and mix in the Perugia sauce. Serve at once.

Salsa alle tre verdura

Three vegetable sauce

Once you have mastered this recipe any combination of vegetables you have to hand will make a good sauce. If you are using eggplants either salt and press them with a weight for an hour then rinse to remove the bitter juices or, if you lack time for this, peel them.

100 ml olive oil
2 cloves garlic, finely chopped
2 tablespoons parsley, finely chopped
2 eggplants, cubed
4 zucchini, cut in rounds
200 g fresh mushrooms, roughly chopped
4 sprigs fresh oregano, chopped (or 1 teaspoon dried)
1 teaspoon salt
pasta (p.84)

Heat the oil in a saucepan and fry the garlic and parsley until the garlic is just turning to a pale gold. Add the eggplant, stirring occasionally. When the eggplant is cooked add the zucchini, mushrooms and oregano. Fry the vegetables stirring continuously and gently scraping any residue from the sides and bottom of the pan as you do. Once the vegetables have been cooked to your satisfaction add the salt and serve with a short pasta, such as *conchiglie*.

Pasta con carciofi

Pasta with artichokes

The artichoke is a most edible thistle. It has its origins probably
along the Barbary coast, but the Italians developed it to become the
aristocrat of all vegetables. Along with a variety of other vegetables
the artichoke was once regarded as an aphrodisiac. Legend would
have us believe that Catherine de Medici, a lady known for her
delight in all foods, ate so many on one occasion she nearly burst.
Jane Grigson writes that 'the artichoke above all is the vegetable
expression of civilized living'. Heady stuff.

Artichokes are readily available. They are a little expensive at
the beginning of the season but quickly reduce in price. Italian
cuisine is responsible for a myriad of recipes using artichokes, but if
you have not tasted them before, try them simply boiled in salted
water, pull off each leaf separately and eat them dipped in melted
butter with a little lemon and garlic. As you become more
adventurous there are numerous ways to handle the vegetable and
certainly in terms of sauces for pasta you can let your imagination
run riot.

> 6 large artichokes
> juice of two lemons
> 75 ml olive oil
> 25 g butter
> 1 small onion, thinly sliced
> 2 cloves garlic, finely chopped
> 1 tablespoon celery, finely chopped
> salt
> black pepper, freshly ground
> *Parmigiano* cheese, freshly grated
> pasta (p.84)

Remove the coarse external leaves from the artichoke and
discard them. Cut the artichokes into quarters lengthwise,
cover and soak in cold water, acidulated with the juice of
lemons, for not less than one hour.

Heat the oil and butter in a saucepan and gently brown
the onion, garlic and celery taking care that the butter does

not burn. Add the artichoke quarters and salt and pepper to taste and cook for thirty minutes stirring frequently. Serve this sauce with a short pasta, such as *penne* or *rigatoni*, and with plenty of *Parmigiano* cheese.

Penne con carciofi
Penne with artichokes

This dish dates back in Italy to Roman times and it is supposed that legionnaires brought it from Palestine. It is another delightful way to combine artichokes with pasta, here using a short pasta such as **penne.**

4 artichokes
100 g bacon, finely chopped
2 tablespoons *Parmigiano* cheese, freshly grated
100 g butter
1 tablespoon parsley, finely chopped
50 ml olive oil
salt
pepper
400 g *penne*

Clean the artichokes by eliminating the tough outer leaves and cutting away the prickly tips. Cut the artichokes into eight sections. Put them in a pan with half the butter and cook over a low flame, adding a few spoonsful of water occasionally so that the artichokes do not dry out. Add salt and pepper to taste. In another pan cook the bacon over a high heat with the olive oil until the bacon is crispy. Cook the *penne* in salted water. Drain and add to it the cooked artichokes and bacon. Sprinkle with parsley and grated *Parmigiano* cheese and the remaining 50 g of melted butter.

Spaghetti ninfetta

Nymphs' spaghetti

Broccoli was a very popular vegetable in Italy in Etruscan, Greek and Roman times. During the Middle Ages it became a food of the masses, not just for the rich. In Emilia-Romagna its ancient splendours are recalled in this sauce, the charmingly named 'nymphs' **spaghetti**'.

> 500 g tomatoes, peeled and deseeded if fresh, sieved
>   if tinned
> 40 g sultanas
> 40 g pine nuts
> 2 cloves garlic, finely chopped
> 1 bunch broccoli
> 1 dessertspoon parsley, finely chopped
> 75 ml olive oil
> salt
> 400 g *spaghetti*

Cook the broccoli for a few minutes. It should retain some firmness. Drain and divide it into small flowerettes. Lightly brown the garlic in oil. Add the tomatoes and cook for ten minutes. Then mix in the sultanas and pine nuts. Cook the *spaghetti* until *al dente*, then strain. Put the *spaghetti* in a serving bowl, add the broccoli flowerettes, sauce and chopped parsley. Mix gently and serve.

Pasta corta in salsa di broccoli

Short pasta with broccoli

This is another delicious winter dish based on broccoli. The vibrant colour of the broccoli against the pasta brightens any table. Be sure to deseed the chilli thoroughly and carefully, then skewer it firmly with two toothpicks inserted diagonally. This will enable you to find and then discard it at the end of cooking. Take great care not to rub the area around eyes or lips with fingers which have handled chilli.

> 75 ml olive oil
> 1 clove garlic, crushed
> 1 red chilli
> 500 g broccoli, cooked
> black pepper, freshly ground
> *pecorino* cheese
> pasta (p.84)

Heat the oil in a large pan, add the garlic and chilli and cook until the garlic has coloured to a pale gold. Adjust the heat to a high flame and add the cooked and well-drained broccoli. Fry briskly for two to three minutes then reduce the heat and cook gently for fifteen minutes. Cook the pasta while the broccoli is being prepared and drain it quickly, allowing some of the water to adhere to the pasta. Pour the pasta into the pan with the broccoli and mix for a few minutes allowing the excess moisture to evaporate. Carefully remove the chilli and sprinkle with pepper and *pecorino* cheese before serving.

Spaghetti marzolini

Springtime sauce

This is a refreshing dish enjoyed in Italy in the springtime. It is so named because March marks the beginning of spring there.

> 500 g asparagus
> 500 g tomatoes, peeled and deseeded if fresh, or
>   sieved if tinned
> 75 ml olive oil
> salt
> pepper
> 400 g *spaghetti*

Wash the asparagus and cut off the hard ends. Heat the oil in a pot, add the asparagus and cook for a few minutes, turning gently so as not to break the asparagus stalks. Add the tomatoes, salt and pepper to taste. Cover and cook for twenty minutes over a low heat. Uncover the pot for the last ten minutes so that some of the liquid can evaporate. Cook the *spaghetti* in boiling, salted water until it is *al dente*. Strain, place it in the serving bowls and ladle the asparagus sauce over it.

Salsa d'estate
Summertime sauce

This is a tangy sauce, which takes its name from the warm colours of the red and yellow capsicums. Take care to remove the bitter juices from the eggplant before cooking either by salting and pressing with weights, followed by rinsing, or by peeling thickly.

> 75 ml olive oil (including the oil from the anchovies)
> 1 small onion, finely sliced
> 2 cloves garlic, finely chopped
> 2 red or yellow capsicums, deseeded and sliced
> 2 eggplants, cubed
> 1 tablespoon parsley, finely chopped
> 1 tin anchovies, chopped
> pasta (p.84)

Heat the oil in a saucepan, add the onion and garlic and cook over moderate heat until both are nicely browned. Add the capsicums and cook for ten minutes, stirring frequently. Add the eggplant and parsley and cook for a further ten minutes, stirring frequently. When the vegetables are cooked add the anchovies and stir the mixture well to distribute them evenly. Cook for a further one to two minutes and serve with a short pasta such as *fusilli*. Remember that the anchovies are quite salty so additional salt is unnecessary.

Bucatini in salsa alla guiliano

Bucatini with julienne sauce

The name of this sauce derives from the way in which a Roman emperor — who took a gluttonous delight in eating vegetables — preferred to have them cut into thin strips. His name was Severus Guiliano and he is better remembered for this contribution to cooking than for other achievements.

6 stalks celery
4 medium carrots
4 potatoes
2 onions or 4 leeks
50 g olive oil
Parmigiano cheese, freshly grated
salt
pepper
300 g *bucatini* or any short pasta to hand

Cut all the vegetables *guiliano* (julienne style), that is, into long, match-like shapes. Sauté the onion and potatoes in oil for about fifteen minutes, add the celery, carrot, salt, pepper and a little water and cook for a further five minutes. Cook the pasta and strain, mix the sauce in gently. If desired, sprinkle with *Parmigiano* cheese. This dish is best eaten with a spoon.

Salsa di cavolini di Brussels

Brussels sprout sauce

This is another economical and easy to prepare sauce. It is a delicious and unusual way to serve a winter vegetable that quite undeservedly seems to be avoided by a large number of people who had it forced upon them when children. This sauce should convert such people. Although packaged crumbs are adequate, try to use home-made breadcrumbs. The result will be far superior.

> 1 kg small Brussels sprouts
> 75 ml olive oil
> 50 g butter
> 100 g breadcrumbs
> 100 g *Parmigiano* cheese, freshly grated
> extra *Parmigiano* cheese, freshly grated
> pasta (p.84)

Trim the Brussels sprouts of any unsightly and tough outer leaves and remove any excess stem. Make a small nick in the bottom of each sprout with a sharp knife to help speed the cooking time, and cook in boiling salted water for seven to ten minutes. The sprouts should be cooked but still firm and should still be green in colour. Drain thoroughly and cut into four, lengthwise.

Heat the oil and butter in a saucepan taking care not to burn the butter. Add the Brussels sprouts, stirring frequently over a high heat until they begin to brown. Now add the breadcrumbs and *Parmigiano* cheese and continue cooking until the breadcrumbs are well browned. Add extra butter if necessary. Serve with a short pasta such as *conchiglie* or *fusilli* and extra *Parmigiano* cheese as required.

Salso di sedano
Celery sauce

The Italians appreciate celery far more than Australians and this
unusual sauce is evidence of that appreciation. It is best to use the
coarse outer stalks for cooking and the delicate white heart for
eating raw; dipped in a little oil and salt the heart is quite delicious.

> 75 ml oil
> 1 small onion, finely sliced
> 1 large stick celery, washed and trimmed and cut into
>   small pieces
> 500 g tomatoes, peeled and deseeded if fresh, or
>   sieved if tinned
> 2 sprigs thyme, chopped
> salt
> black pepper, freshly ground
> Parmigiano cheese, freshly grated
> pasta (p.84)

Heat the oil in a saucepan and fry the onion and celery over
moderate heat until they become golden in colour. Add the
tomatoes, thyme, salt and pepper and let the sauce simmer
gently for fifteen minutes. Serve with a short pasta like penne
or fusilli and plenty of Parmigiano cheese.

112

Fettucine alla cipolle

Fettucine with onions

This is a dish from the Piedmont region. Basically a simple onion sauce, it is given a dash of colour by the use of the tomato paste.

4 medium onions, thinly sliced
100 ml olive oil
50 ml tomato paste
salt
pepper
Parmigiano cheese, freshly grated
400 g *fettucine*

Peel and slice the onions. Boil the onion rings in salted water for a few minutes over a low heat. Strain and put in a pan with olive oil. Cook, covered, until the onions are transparent. Add the tomato paste together with salt and pepper to taste. Combine the onion sauce with the *fettucine*, cook until *al dente*, sprinkle with *Parmigiano* cheese and serve.

Pasta con le melanzane

Pasta with eggplant

This is a modern version of a very ancient recipe, known as
Leganum, which dates back to Roman times.

> 250 g tomato sauce (pp.84-5)
> 4 eggplants, washed and sliced
> 1 *mozzarella* cheese
> 1 tablespoon butter
> 2 tablespoons *Parmigiano* cheese, freshly grated
> salt
> pepper
> 300 g *macaroni*

Wash and slice the eggplants crosswise into rounds. Heat the
oil in a pan and fry the eggplant slices until they are golden.
Remove the eggplant slices from the pan, dry them on a
paper towel and sprinkle with salt and pepper. Cook the
macaroni until it is *al dente*. Strain and mix it with the tomato
sauce. Slice the *mozzarella* cheese. In a casserole dish put a
layer of *macaroni*, another of eggplant and another of
mozzarella; top with *macaroni*. Add grated *Parmigiano* cheese
and dot with butter. Heat the casserole in a moderate oven
for about twenty minutes.

Broccoletti di rapa con conchiglie
Turnip tops with shell pasta

This sauce originates from the region of Puglia in southern Italy. It is seldom made elsewhere in the country, except by people who were born in Puglia. Don't be deterred: it is delicious and unusual.

1 kg turnip tops
6 anchovy fillets, finely chopped
2 cloves garlic, crushed
75 ml olive oil
salt
500 g shell pasta

Wash the turnip tops well under running water and drain. Cut the stalks in small pieces. The leaves should remain whole. Have ready a large pot of boiling, salted water. Toss in the leaves and chopped stalks of the turnips. After about five minutes add the shell pasta and cook until it is *al dente*. The turnip tops should also be cooked at this point. Strain well to eliminate any excess water and set aside for the moment. In a large pan sauté the crushed garlic and the chopped anchovy fillets in oil for a few minutes, then add the pasta and turnip tops. Mix well. Simmer for about ten minutes to give all the flavours time to blend, then serve hot.

Spaghetti al finocchio

Spaghetti with fennel

This is a very ancient recipe from Lombardy. The vividly coloured saffron spice had been introduced into Europe by the Venetians.

> 2 bulbs fennel, cleaned
> 1 onion, finely chopped
> 50 ml olive oil
> 1 tablespoon pine nuts
> 1 teaspoon saffron
> salt
> pepper
> 400 g *spaghetti*

Clean the fennel bulbs, cut off the hard tops and leaves. Put them in a pot of boiling salted water and cook until quite tender. Drain. Keep the fennel water. Chop up the onion and fennel and sauté for a few minutes in a pot with the oil. Add saffron mixed with a little hot water, salt and pepper to taste. Turn off the heat and add the pine nuts. Bring the fennel water to the boil and cook the *spaghetti* in it until *al dente*. Strain the pasta, mix it with the fennel sauce and serve.

Maccheroni alla olive

Macaroni with olives

This is a relatively modern dish, which belongs to the cuisine of Tuscany.

> 1 glass milk
> 1 tablespoon butter
> 1 tablespoon parsley, finely chopped
> 4 tablespoons *Parmigiano*, freshly grated
> 2 eggs
> 100 g stuffed olives
> salt
> pepper
> 400 g *maccheroni*

Beat the eggs in a bowl, add butter (which should have been cut into small pieces), the *Parmigiano*, parsley, milk, salt and pepper to taste. Mix well. Cook the *maccheroni* in boiling, salted water until *al dente*. Strain. Put the pasta on a warmed serving plate, pour over the prepared egg mixture, toss well and top with sliced olives.

Tagliatelle con salsa di noci

Tagliatelle with walnut sauce

This is another specialty of Naples, where the best walnuts in Italy are grown.

> 250 g walnuts, shelled
> 3 cloves garlic, crushed
> 1 slice bread
> 150 g butter
> milk
> salt
> 300 g *tagliatelle*

Cover the slice of bread with milk and let it soak. Chop the walnuts and garlic finely or crush them with a mortar and pestle if you have one. Lift the bread out of the milk without squeezing it excessively. Put the bread in a bowl with the walnut and garlic mixture, add salt, combine thoroughly and let the sauce stand for a while before use. Cook the *tagliatelle*, strain, add butter then fold in the walnut sauce.

Salsa di funghi

Mushroom sauce

Field mushrooms are best suited to this recipe. Make sure they are wiped carefully with a damp cloth and check that the gills are not harbouring any small insects.

> 100 ml olive oil
> 3 cloves garlic, finely chopped
> ½ onion, finely chopped
> 1 sprig rosemary
> 3 tablespoons parsley, finely chopped
> 500 g mushrooms, cleaned and thinly sliced
> salt
> black pepper, freshly ground
> pasta (p.84)

Heat the oil in a saucepan and evenly brown the garlic and onion over moderate heat. Strip the rosemary leaves from the stalk, chop them together with the parsley and add them with the mushrooms to the onion and garlic. The whole rosemary stalk can be added, too, to extract as much flavour as possible, and then discarded at the end of cooking. Cover the saucepan, and simmer for thirty minutes. A tablespoon or so of broth can be added if you feel the sauce is becoming dry.

Add salt and pepper to taste and serve with a long wide pasta such as *pappardelle*.

Capelli d'angelo con funghi
Angel's hair with mushrooms

Angel's hair is one of the many romantic names with which Italians have christened their varieties of pasta. The pasta is long and very thin and suits this fine mushroom sauce.

50 ml olive oil
½ small onion, finely sliced
1 small hot red chilli, deseeded and finely chopped
100 g *prosciutto*, chopped
500 g mushrooms, wiped clean and thinly sliced
1 kg tomatoes, peeled and deseeded if fresh, or sieved
   if tinned
pasta (p.84)

Heat the oil in a saucepan, add the onion and cook over moderate heat until golden brown. Add the chilli and *prosciutto*. Cook gently for two to three minutes before adding the mushrooms. Cook for a further five minutes. Add the tomatoes and simmer covered for thirty minutes, stirring occasionally. Toss the angel's hair very gently in the sauce and serve immediately.

Salsa alla boscaiola

Bushman's sauce

This sauce is most popular in the mountainous regions of Italy where mushrooms are plentiful.

> 500 g fresh mushrooms, thinly sliced
> 75 ml olive oil
> 1 small onion, finely sliced
> 1 clove garlic, finely chopped
> 500 g tomatoes, peeled and deseeded if fresh, or
>   sieved if tinned
> salt
> black pepper, freshly ground
> pasta (p.84)

Do not wash the mushrooms, but remove any soil from them with a damp cloth and slice thinly. Heat the oil in a saucepan, add the onion and garlic and cook over medium heat to a golden brown. Add the mushrooms and cook for five minutes, stirring frequently. Add the tomatoes, salt and pepper. Cover and simmer gently for thirty minutes. This sauce goes well with *fettucine*.

Funghi alla crema
Mushroom cream sauce

*This is a delicately flavoured cream sauce quite different from the heartier **salsa alla boscaiola** (p. 121). It is quick and easy to make but like all cream sauces it waits for no man and must be served immediately it is ready. The smallest, firmest mushrooms available are the most suitable. Fresh tarragon will give a unique aroma and flavour to the sauce but a good quality dried herb is adequate if this is unavailable.*

> 150 g butter
> 1 kg fresh button mushrooms, finely sliced
> 2 sprigs tarragon, chopped
> salt
> black pepper, freshly ground
> 500 ml cream
> 2 tablespoons parsley, chopped
> *Parmigiano* cheese, freshly grated
> pasta (p.84)

Do not wash the mushrooms, but remove any soil from them with a damp cloth and slice thinly. Melt the butter in a large saucepan and sauté the mushrooms and tarragon over a brisk flame, but taking great care that the butter does not burn. When most of the liquid has evaporated add the salt, pepper, cream and parsley. Over a moderate heat let the mixture bubble until it has thickened. Add a well-drained pasta such as *pappardelle*, cooked *al dente*, and toss it gently with the sauce. Serve immediately with plenty of *Parmigiano* cheese.

Tagliatelle gratinate ai funghi

Tagliatelle gratin with mushrooms

Mushrooms are most often used as a salad vegetable in Australia. Added to a sauce however, they impart a delicate flavour, as in this recipe. You can either use fresh or dried mushrooms. If the latter, remember that they have to be soaked, strained, and the water added to the sauce.

400 g mushrooms, finely sliced
200 g cream
120 g butter
30 g bacon or *pancetta*, finely chopped
6 tablespoons *Parmigiano* cheese, freshly grated
70 g *prosciutto* ham, cut in cubes
½ glass dry white wine
1 small onion, finely chopped
75 ml olive oil
salt
pepper
500 g *tagliatelle*

Cut the onion and bacon finely. Cook them in a pan with 20 g of butter. Add the *prosciutto*, cut in cubes, and olive oil. Gently sauté until the onion is golden and the bacon fat has melted. Clean the mushrooms, slice finely and add to the pan. Mix well. Pour in the wine a little at a time. Add salt and pepper to taste. Cook for 15-20 minutes, stirring in the cream towards the end. Cook the *tagliatelle* in salted water until it is *al dente*, then strain. Have at hand a large, warmed bowl where you can mix the *tagliatelle* with 70 g of butter, four tablespoons of *Parmigiano* cheese and the mushroom sauce. When this is done, pour into a buttered casserole dish. Top with the remaining cheese and butter. Cook in a hot oven for about ten minutes or until a light golden crust has formed.

Salsa di fagioli

Kidney bean sauce

This is a different version of **salsa di sedano**. Other varieties of bean may be used if kidney beans are unavailable. **Salsa di fagioli** needs to cook slowly for a long time to allow the full flavour of the beans to be released. It cannot be successfully hurried.

100 ml olive oil
30 g onion, finely sliced
50 g celery, finely chopped
80 g *pancetta* (or bacon), chopped
½ Italian pork sausage, skinned and finely chopped
2 cloves garlic, finely chopped
1 tablespoon parsley, finely chopped
500 g kidney beans
2 litres water
1 sprig fresh rosemary
Parmigiano cheese, freshly grated
pasta (p.84)

If you are using dried beans soak them overnight in salted water.

Heat the oil in a saucepan and cook the onion, celery, *pancetta* and sausage over high heat until the onion is a golden brown. Add the garlic and parsley and cook for a minute longer. Add all the remaining ingredients and bring to the boil. Reduce the heat quickly and cook uncovered over the lowest possible heat for two hours. Serve with *fettucine*. The addition of *Parmigiano* cheese is optional.

Ragu di fagioli
Kidney bean ragout

This sauce takes on a dark reddish colour from its kidney bean base which, apart from being aesthetically pleasing, is rich in protein. Other beans may be used if kidney beans are unavailable, but you will have a different, although not unpleasant, sauce.

The continental sausages can be skinned easily if you run them under a little cold water. Make a shallow incision along the length of the sausage and then slide the casing off. It is best to mince them with a heavy cook's knife. Run the blade of the knife through the gas jet a few times and you will find that not only do you have a sterile knife but that the meat will not stick to the blade. You may need to repeat this heating process once or twice as you mince the meat.

50 ml olive oil
½ small onion, finely sliced
1 clove garlic, finely chopped
1 tablespoon celery, finely chopped
2 continental sausages, skinned and minced
500 g tomatoes, peeled and deseeded if fresh, or
   sieved if tinned
500 g *borlotti* or kidney beans
2-3 leaves basil, chopped
salt
black pepper, finely ground
pasta (p.84)

Soak the beans overnight in salted water if you are using the dried variety or rinse and drain the tinned beans before use.

Heat the oil in a saucepan and fry the onion, garlic and celery until golden brown. Add the sausage and, stirring frequently, cook until browned. Add the tomatoes and beans and gently cook, covered, for thirty minutes. Add the basil leaves and salt and pepper to taste and serve hot with a long pasta such as *fettucine*.

125

Sugo paesano all'Amatriciana

The true Amatriciana sauce

This is a strongly flavoured sauce named after Amatrice, near Rome, where it originated. It is best served with a short hollow pasta such as **rigatoni**. As the Amatriciana is a rich sauce it is best followed by a main course of lightly cooked white meat or fish.

100 ml olive oil
1 small onion, finely chopped
300 g *pancetta* (or bacon), finely chopped
1 small hot red chilli
500 g tomatoes, peeled and seeded if fresh, or sieved if tinned
100 g *pecorino* cheese, freshly grated
pasta (p.84)

Heat the oil in a saucepan over moderate heat and evenly brown the onions. Cut the *pancetta* or bacon into small cubes of about 1 centimetre, and add to the onions. Reduce the heat a little and cook for two to three minutes before adding the chilli and tomatoes. The hot chilli must be thoroughly and carefully deseeded and then skewered diagonally with two toothpicks to facilitate its removal from the sauce at the end of cooking time.

Cook slowly for twenty to thirty minutes to allow the full flavours to develop. Discard the chilli and serve with short pasta topped generously with *pecorino* cheese.

Tagliatelle con la besciamella

Tagliatelle with white sauce

This recipe is easy to prepare and is a favourite in the region of Emilia-Romagna. In Australia 'white sauce' has frequently meant a grey, lumpy stodge usually used to cover a multitude of overcooked sins. This **besciamella** *is about as far from that image as it is possible to go.*

> **BESCIAMELLA SAUCE**
> 50 g butter
> 50 g flour
> 1 litre milk
>
> 100 g button mushrooms, wiped clean and finely sliced
> 150 g *prosciutto*, cut in strips
> 100 g butter
> *Parmigiano* cheese, freshly grated
> pasta (p.84)

Melt the butter in a saucepan, add the flour, mix it with the butter and cook this roux slowly for five minutes. Do not allow the roux to brown. Have the milk warmed through; pour it all into the saucepan and mix it in with a balloon whisk. Simmer the sauce very slowly for thirty minutes; make sure that it is lump free. Set the *besciamella* aside and keep it warm.

Just before you put the *tagliatelle* on to cook add the sliced mushrooms and *prosciutto* to the *besciamella*. Cook the *tagliatelle* until *al dente* and drain well. Melt the butter into the bottom of a large serving bowl, add the *tagliatelle*, the *besciamella*, plenty of *Parmigiano* cheese and mix gently but thoroughly. Serve at once with extra *Parmigiano*.

Crema alla Gorgonzola
Gorgonzola sauce

This sauce is quick and easy to make. It is quite delicious and even those who swear they cannot stand the sight or smell of any blue cheese, let alone **Gorgonzola**, are usually quickly converted. Accompanied by champagne, it is a delicious start to any meal.

> 150 g butter
> 150 g cream
> 100 g *Gorgonzola* cheese (crust removed)
> pasta (p.84)

Melt the butter in a small saucepan over a medium flame. Add the cream and Gorgonzola which you have cut into small cubes, reduce the heat and cook, stirring continuously, until the cheese has melted completely and the three ingredients have amalgamated. Keep stirring the sauce until it assumes the quality of thick cream. This should take about five minutes.

Use *crema alla Gorgonzola* only with an absorbent pasta such as *tagliatelle* or with *gnocchi* on pp.37-8.

As with all the recipes in this book *crema alla Gorgonzola* can be adapted to other ingredients, the most well-known and popular variation being *ai quattro formaggio*. The recipe for *Penne ai quatro formaggi* is given on page 130. Another way of serving this dish is to use the four different cheeses to prepare four different sauces. Toss equal quantities of *gnocchi* in each sauce and present each person with four small serves of differently sauced *gnocchi* on the one plate. This method of serving can sometimes lead to a visual catastrophe which to say the least is unappetising, so take care not to overload the plate. It is much better to have your guests asking for seconds than to watch them struggling through a mountain of food.

We would suggest a variety of *Gorgonzola*, Emmenthal, Edam and *Parmigiano* but the combinations are infinite and it is up to your personal preferences to choose the cheeses you like and feel are compatible with each other and with the remainder of the meal. Remember to think of colour as well as flavour when making your decision. Having settled this, just follow the basic recipe substituting the cheeses of your choice for the *Gorgonzola*.

Pasta con ricotta

Pasta with ricotta cheese

It is hard to think of a simpler or more satisfying dish than this. Based on a traditional shepherd's meal, the ingredients are those the shepherd would have to hand or could easily carry. A short pasta such as **maccheroni** *would be the most traditionally appropriate. Freshly made* **ricotta** *cheese, now available in Italian delicatessens and many supermarkets, gives the most agreeable result, although packaged* **ricotta** *will do.*

> 300 g fresh *ricotta* cheese
> 100 g *Parmigiano* cheese, freshly grated
> black pepper, freshly ground
> pasta (p.84)

Cut or crumble the *ricotta* and add it to the cooked pasta. Top with plenty of *Parmigiano* or *pecorino* cheese, and have a peppermill to hand.

Penne ai quatro formaggi
Penne with four cheeses

This is another creation of the great cuisine of Parma. You will find that in the cooking the flavours of the cheeses will richly and unexpectedly combine.

> 60 g mozzarella
> 60 g Parmigiano
> 60 g gruyère
> 60 g edam
> All the cheeses should be finely sliced in ribbons
> 80 g Parmigiano (additional), freshly grated
> 100 g butter
> 400 g penne

Cook the penne in salted water until it is al dente, strain well and return it to the cooking pot. Quickly add the ribbons of cheese, 50 g of melted butter and half of the grated Parmigiano cheese. Mix briskly. Pour into a pre-heated casserole dish and cover with the remaining butter and Parmigiano cheese. Serve immediately.

Penne al pepe e pecorino
Penne with pepper and pecorino

This is a sauce from the Rome region which can be prepared quickly and is enjoyed by those with a taste for hot, spicy food. Remember to be generous with the pepper.

> 200 g pecorino cheese, freshly grated
> 1 tablespoon black pepper, freshly ground
> 500 g penne

Grate the cheese and grind the pepper while waiting for the pasta to cook until al dente. Then strain the pasta and mix with the pepper and cheese. Serve at once.

Bucatini del pastore

Shepherd's pasta

This is another traditional shepherd's dish and is quick and easy to prepare as well as very nutritious. As with **Pasta con ricotta** you will obtain a better flavour if you are able to use fresh **ricotta**.

> 50 g *bucatini* (p.84)
> 250 g fresh *ricotta*
> 100 g butter
> black pepper, freshly ground or 1 small hot red chilli, deseeded and crushed

Put the *bucatini* on to cook in boiling salted water. While it is cooking, mix all the other ingredients with two tablespoons of the *bucatini* cooking water. When the pasta is cooked, drain well and mix gently with the cheese mixture.

Salsa alla mozzarella

Mozzarella sauce

A light sauce combining two complementary cheeses. This is an ideal dish to prepare as a quick and sustaining snack.

> 400 g *spaghettini* (p.84)
> 150 g butter
> 80 g *Parmigiano* cheese, freshly grated
> 200 g *mozzarella*, thinly sliced
> a little milk

Break the lengths of *spaghettini* in half and cook in plenty of boiling salted water until *al dente*. Drain well and mix the butter and 50 grams of the *Parmigiano* cheese into the hot pasta. Tip the *spaghettini* mixture into a well-buttered casserole and top with the sliced *mozzarella*, and the remainder of the *Parmigiano* cheese. Pour over a little milk and bake in a hot oven until the *mozzarella* melts. Serve very hot.

Salsa di mollica di pane

Breadcrumb sauce

This sauce is an extremely economical one and quite delicious. Bought breadcrumbs can be used successfully but home-made breadcrumbs made from stale bread make a far better sauce. Use the 'heart' of the loaf, not the crust, when making the breadcrumbs.

> 250 ml olive oil
> 2 cloves garlic, finely chopped
> 2 sprigs of rosemary, chopped
> 1 cup of breadcrumbs
> *pecorino* cheese, freshly grated
> pasta (p.84)

Heat 100 ml of the oil in a saucepan over a high flame and cook the garlic and rosemary until the garlic is pale gold. Reduce the heat to moderate and add the remaining oil and breadcrumbs. Cook until the breadcrumbs are a dark golden brown, stirring the sauce continuously as the crumbs will otherwise burn very quickly. Serve the sauce with a short pasta such as *fusilli* or *conchiglie* and with plenty of *pecorino* cheese.

Salsa all'Americana

American sauce

This is a universally known and liked dish. The ingredients are more expensive than for many other pasta dishes and this, combined with the fact that at one time all things American were associated with wealth, gives this sauce its name.

Salsa all'Americana is usually served with **spaghetti** because this was the pasta with which Americans were first familiar. However, you may use virtually any variety of pasta you choose.

> **SMALL MEATBALLS**
> 400 g minced lean veal and pork
> 1 small onion, finely chopped
> 1 tablespoon parsley, finely chopped
> 2 cloves garlic, crushed
> 2 eggs
> 100 g *Parmigiano* cheese, freshly grated
> 2 tablespoons breadcrumbs
>
> *Salsa di pomodoro* (pp.84-5)
> 500 g *spaghetti*

Put all the ingredients for the meatballs in the food processor and mix them thoroughly. Shape the mixture into balls about the size of a small walnut. Fry the meatballs in a little oil until they are nicely browned all over. Drain them on absorbent kitchen paper while you prepare the *salsa di pomodoro* which is on pp.84-5.

After this sauce has cooked for twenty minutes add the meatballs and simmer gently for thirty minutes. Remove the meatballs from the sauce and keep them warm while you toss the pasta in the *salsa di pomodoro*. Serve the pasta on individual plates and distribute the meatballs equitably. Have plenty of *Parmigiano* cheese available to sprinkle over them.

La vera Bolognese

Classic Bolognese sauce

Like **salsa di pomodoro**, there are numerous versions of
Bolognese sauce. Australians tend to be familiar with a bland,
simplified sauce of minced beef and tomatoes but the traditional
Bolognese is far from this, being quite rich and sweet from long
slow cooking and good quality and fresh ingredients. If you prefer
an even richer sauce than the one below add half a cup of cream
and a knob of butter just before the end of cooking time. A sauce
which is richer again can be obtained by adding lightly fried
chopped chicken livers and mushrooms, but this will no longer be a
Bolognese sauce. Or, let your imagination take over.

    Bolognese can be served with almost any pasta although it is
said that a marriage of **tagliatelle** and **Bolognese** is one made in
heaven. It is equally good with **rigatoni** or **gnocchi** and is an
indispensable part of **lasagne**.

> 50 g butter
> 50 ml olive oil
> 30 g onion, finely sliced
> 1 stalk celery, finely chopped
> 1 medium carrot, finely chopped
> 100 g *pancetta* or *prosciutto* (or bacon if the others
>   are unobtainable), finely sliced
> 200 g lean pork, finely chopped
> 200 g lean veal, finely chopped
> 50 g Italian sausage, skinned and finely chopped
> ½ glass dry white wine
> 1 kg tomatoes, peeled and deseeded if fresh, or sieved
>   if tinned
> water (optional)
> pasta (p.84)

Heat the butter and oil in a large pan, deeper than it is wide
(to stop the sauce reducing too quickly). Taking care that
the butter does not burn, fry the onion, celery, carrot and
pancetta or *prosciutto* until the onion is evenly browned. Add

the chopped meats and fry them very lightly, cooking them only until they have lost their raw look. Moisten with the wine and increase the heat at once, stirring occasionally until all the wine has reduced. Add the tomatoes and a little water if you feel the mixture is too thick. Once the sauce starts to bubble again, turn down the heat to the barest simmer. Cook uncovered for two and a half to three hours, stirring occasionally. Taste and add salt if you feel it necessary, bearing in mind that the sauce should be sweet in the Emilia-Romagna tradition.

Should you wish to make any additions to the sauce they should be made after the wine has reduced.

Salsa d'abbacchio e peperoni

Spring lamb and capsicum sauce

Australia has such a good supply of spring lamb it is a shame that we are sometimes rather blasé in our treatment of it. This is a different way of making the most of it.

> 200 g lamb, trimmed and cut into small pieces
> salt
> black pepper, freshly ground
> 125 ml olive oil
> 2 cloves garlic, finely chopped
> 2 bay leaves
> 150 ml dry white wine
> 500 g tomatoes, peeled and deseeded if fresh, or
>   sieved if tinned
> 2 capsicums, deseeded and finely chopped
> pasta (p.84)

Sprinkle the lamb with a little salt and freshly ground black pepper and put aside for the moment.

Heat the oil in a saucepan over medium heat and add the garlic and bay leaves, cooking until the garlic is a pale gold. Add the lamb and brown it evenly, stirring occasionally. Add the white wine and let it reduce completely.

Mix in the tomatoes and capsicum, reduce the heat and slowly simmer, covered, for one and a half hours, stirring from time to time. Should the sauce become too thick add a little broth or water. Serve with a wide pasta such as *pappardelle*.

Salsa di pollo

Chicken sauce

This sauce has a delicate flavour and makes a good entrée before a stronger tasting main course. Any other poultry can be substituted for the chicken with good results.

75 ml olive oil
1 small onion, finely chopped
2 cloves garlic, finely chopped
2 continental sausages, skinned and minced
½ chicken, boned and cut into large cubes
500 g tomatoes, peeled and deseeded if fresh, or
  sieved if tinned
1 tablespoon parsley, finely chopped
salt
black pepper, freshly ground
pasta (p.84)

Heat the oil in a saucepan and carefully brown the onion and garlic over high heat. Add the minced sausages and cook for ten minutes stirring frequently. Add the chicken pieces, brown them quickly. Add the tomatoes, parsley, salt and pepper. Bring to the boil then reduce the heat and simmer uncovered for thirty minutes. Serve hot with *tagliatelle* or *fettucine*.

Salsa allo stile Modenese

Sauce Modenese style

*This is a fine, rich sauce that goes well with fresh **tagliatelle**. It makes a perfect start to a good meal but do remember when you plan the rest of your menu that it is rich and quite filling. Like all cream sauces the **Modenese** will not wait happily, so make sure everybody is ready to eat before you start cooking.*

> 150 g fresh peas
> 250 g butter
> 100 g *prosciutto*, cut in strips
> 100 g cream
> **Parmigiano** cheese, freshly grated
> pasta (p.84)

Cook the peas as you like but making sure that they retain their bright colour and are not overcooked. Set them aside.

Melt the butter in a saucepan and lightly fry the *prosciutto*. Add the peas and stir briskly. Pour in the cream and let it bubble and thicken slightly. Add the well-drained cooked *tagliatelle* and toss it gently with the sauce, distributing the peas and *prosciutto* evenly. Serve immediately with *Parmigiano* cheese.

Spaghetti alla carbonara

Coal vendors' spaghetti

This is a sauce whose name is very familiar to Australians, though they may not know that **carbonara** refers to coal vendors, and that in consequence the dish receives a final dusting of freshly ground black pepper to simulate coal dust. As the **salsa alla carbonara** is egg-based it is not appropriate to serve an egg pasta with it. Use a pasta such as **spaghetti** that has been made without eggs.

> 25 ml olive oil
> 150 g bacon, cut into small squares
> 4 eggs
> 4 tablespoons cream
> 50 g *Parmigiano* cheese, freshly grated
> salt
> 50 g butter
> black pepper, freshly ground
> extra *Parmigiano* cheese, freshly grated
> pasta (p.84)

Heat the oil in a small frying pan, add the bacon and cook gently until it is golden brown. Set it aside while you prepare the rest of the sauce.

Beat the eggs, cream, cheese and salt in a bowl, combining them well. Melt the butter in a large saucepan until it is foaming and beginning to brown. It can burn at this point so be careful. Add the bacon and egg mixture to the pan, stir it well and remove from the heat. Add the cooked and well-drained pasta to the pot and toss it quickly and carefully in the sauce, distributing the bacon evenly. Serve immediately with a liberal dusting of black pepper and extra *Parmigiano* cheese.

Spaghetti mimosa

Spaghetti with mimosa sauce

This sauce takes its name from the colour imparted by the saffron and curry powders, which suggest the mimosa flower. It is a typical sauce of the northern part of Emilia-Romagna, around the area of Parma. It is a delicate sauce which can be made quickly and it should be served with any type of long pasta.

> 200 g cream
> 100 g *prosciutto* or cooked ham, finely sliced
> 2 egg yolks, beaten
> ½ teaspoon saffron powder
> 1 teaspoon curry powder
> 4 tablespoons *Parmigiano* cheese, freshly grated
> salt
> 400 g *spaghetti*

Cook the *spaghetti* in boiling, salted water until it is *al dente*. While the pasta is cooking, prepare the mimosa sauce in the following way: slice the ham and place it in a pan with cream and the grated *Parmigiano* cheese. Cook over a low flame. Mix the saffron and curry powders with a little hot water (some of the water used for cooking the pasta will do) and add to the sauce. Stir well and cook until the sauce comes to the boil. Remove the pan from the heat and add the two beaten egg yolks. Then serve with *spaghetti*.

Bucatini con cacio e uova

Bucatini with cheese and eggs

This is a typical recipe of the Ligurian region, though versions of it can be found in other parts of Italy. Cheap to make, it shows that such recipes are likely to be found in the most far-flung places.

150 g butter
50 g *Parmigiano* cheese, freshly grated
25 g *pecorino* cheese, freshly grated
3 eggs
2 tablespoons mixed basil and parsley, finely chopped
salt
pepper
400 g *bucatini*

Break the *bucatini* into 8cm lengths and cook it in boiling, lightly salted water until *al dente*, then strain. Melt the butter in a large pan and tip in the *bucatini*. Remove the pan from the heat. Add the two cheeses, basil and parsley and plenty of ground black pepper. Beat the eggs with a pinch of salt, pour them on to the pasta and mix well. Return to a low heat until the eggs coagulate, then serve.

Salsa di fegatini
Chicken liver sauce

This is a Venetian sauce and very rich and filling. The cooked chicken livers have the consistency of pâté so a short pasta like **bucatini** is most suitable. If you are using this sauce for a first course do not follow with anything rich or heavy.

50 ml olive oil
100 g butter
1 small onion, finely chopped
1 sprig fresh rosemary, stalk discarded and leaves
    chopped
200 g chicken livers, chopped
500 g tomatoes, peeled and deseeded if fresh, or
    sieved if tinned
salt
black pepper, freshly ground
Parmigiano cheese, freshly grated
pasta (p.84)

Heat the oil and butter in a saucepan. Add the onion and rosemary and cook until the onion is golden brown. Take care that the butter does not burn. Add the chicken livers and cook, stirring frequently until they lose their rawness. Add the tomatoes, salt and pepper and simmer uncovered for fifteen to twenty minutes. Serve with plenty of *Parmigiano* cheese.

142

Tagliatelle con fegatini
Tagliatelle with chicken livers

Venice is noted for its marvellous fish dishes, but another of its specialities is liver, done in many ways, of which this is one of the most satisfying.

> 100 g chicken livers
> 3 continental sausages, skinned and finely chopped
> 50 g pork lard, cut into small pieces
> rosemary, sage, bay leaves, small quantities of each,
>   finely chopped
> 100 g tomatoes, peeled and deseeded if fresh, or
>   sieved if tinned
> salt
> pepper
> pecorino cheese, freshly grated
> 500 g tagliatelle

Put the chicken livers in a pot of boiling water for a couple of minutes, then strain and cut them into pieces which should not be too small. Melt the lard in a pan and add herbs and the chicken livers, then — after a few minutes — the sausages as well. Cook until the sausages have begun to brown, then tip in the tomatoes, add salt and pepper to taste. Stirring occasionally, let the sauce cook for about fifteen minutes. Cook the tagliatelle until al dente in salted water. Strain and mix with the chicken liver sauce. If desired, top with grated pecorino cheese.

Salsa all'arrabbiata
'Wild' pasta sauce

The origins of this exciting name remain a culinary mystery. The **arrabbiata** *is a strong and tangy flavour and is best served with a short pasta such as* **fusilli** *or* **penne.**

> 100 g butter
> 2 cloves garlic, finely chopped
> 1 small hot red chilli, carefully deseeded and chopped
> 150 g bacon, cut into small cubes
> 300 g mushrooms, wiped clean and thinly sliced
> 500 g tomatoes, peeled and deseeded if fresh, or
>   sieved if tinned
> 2 sprigs fresh basil, chopped
> salt
> *Parmigiano* or *pecorino* cheese, freshly grated
> pasta (p.84)

Melt the butter in a saucepan, add the garlic and chilli and cook until the garlic is pale golden. Take care that the butter does not burn. Add the bacon and cook over moderate heat for five minutes. Next add the mushrooms and cook for a further five minutes before adding the tomatoes, basil and salt to taste. Cook covered, stirring occasionally, for twenty minutes. Serve with plenty of *Parmigiano* or *pecorino* cheese.

Salsa di quaglie
Quail sauce

Variations on this sauce are numerous: it lends itself to all game so try it with hare, pheasant, pigeon, squab or guinea fowl. Although game is quite expensive in Australia this sauce is still economical: the sauce dresses a pasta course and the quail (or other game) is removed from the sauce and eaten as a separate course later.

> 75 ml olive oil
> ½ small onion, finely chopped
> 2 cloves garlic, finely chopped
> 100 g bacon, diced
> 6 quails (1 per person), cleaned and cut in quarters
> 500 g tomatoes, peeled and deseeded if fresh, or sieved if tinned
> 1 sprig fresh sage, coarsely chopped
> salt
> black pepper, freshly ground
> pasta (p.84)

Heat the oil in a saucepan and evenly brown the onion and garlic. Add the bacon and quarters of quail and brown well, taking care that you do not allow any of the ingredients to burn. Add the tomatoes, sage, salt and pepper and mix well. Bring to the boil, reduce the heat and slowly simmer the sauce, uncovered, for thirty minutes. Remove the quails. (Though their juices have flavoured the sauce the quails should not be dry and can be eaten as a separate dish.) This delicately flavoured sauce goes well with *tagliatelle* or *fettucine*.

Salsa di coniglio
Rabbit sauce

In Australia rabbits are readily available and cheap to buy, although we do not seem to take the best advantage of this. Try them in this sauce which has a strong flavour and goes well with a good red wine. Should you wish, the recipe can be adapted for all types of game.

> 100 ml olive oil
> 1 clove garlic, finely chopped
> 2 small onions, finely chopped
> 50 g pancetta (or bacon), finely chopped
> plain flour
> 1 whole rabbit, jointed
> 150 ml dry red wine
> 4 cloves
> pinch cinnamon
> salt
> black pepper, freshly ground
> 50 g butter
> pasta (p.84)

Heat the oil in a large saucepan over a high flame, add the onions, garlic and pancetta and cook until pale golden. Dust the rabbit pieces lightly with flour and add them to the saucepan and brown evenly, turning the meat when necessary. Add the red wine, cloves, cinnamon, salt and pepper, stirring the sauce well, and cook over moderate heat for one to one and a half hours (depending on the toughness or tenderness of the rabbit). Add the butter at the end of cooking and swirl it into the sauce. Serve immediately with a pasta of your choice.

Capelli d'angelo al salmone

Angel's hair with smoked salmon

This is a rich and glamorous start to any meal and a good way either to stretch a leftover scrap of smoked salmon or your weekly budget if you are feeling poor but want to treat yourself and your guests. Serve with iced champagne.

> 500 g capelli d'angelo
> 150 g butter
> 150 g cream
> 100 g good quality smoked salmon, cut into thin strips
> pasta (p.84)

Melt the butter over low heat and add the cream. Cook slowly, stirring continuously for ten minutes until the cream-butter mixture has thickened to the consistency of thick cream. Add the slivers of smoked salmon and toss immediately with already cooked *capelli d'angelo* pasta.

Salsa Buranella

Sauce of Burano

Many Italian pasta dishes which are based on seafood are named not **marinara**, but after the towns or regions where they are made. This sauce comes from Burano, one of the islands near Venice. When making this sauce it is essential to have all the ingredients prepared beforehand. The fish cooks very quickly and will not wait for you. The choice of seafood is optional; use what is freshest at the market but always try to include some shellfish.

This sauce is very substantial and quite rich, therefore serve it with any pasta not made with eggs.

> 75 ml olive oil
> 100 g butter
> 2 cloves garlic, crushed
> 150 g squid, cut in rings
> 300 g prawns, shelled and cleaned thoroughly, cut in half
> 200 g whitebait
> 500 g mussels, cooked covered in a little water over high heat until they open and then removed from their shells
> 100 ml fish broth (p.48)
> 100 ml dry white wine
> 500 g tomatoes, peeled and deseeded if fresh, or sieved if tinned
> 2 tablespoons parsley, finely chopped
> salt
> black pepper, freshly ground
> pasta (p.84)

Heat the oil and butter in a saucepan and fry the garlic until it is pale gold. Take care that the butter does not burn. Add the squid and cook for five minutes stirring from time to time. Now at three minute intervals add the prawns, whitebait and mussels. Increase the heat and add the fish broth. Bring quickly to the boil then reduce the heat and simmer for five minutes. Add the white wine and continue cooking for a further ten minutes. Add the tomatoes, parsley, salt and pepper and cook for ten minutes more.

Serve hot with pasta of your choice.

Salsa di vongole e cappe sante

Clam and scallop sauce

This sauce has a quite beautiful pearly white hue and a most delicious and delicate flavour. As with all seafood sauces remember that you have to eat the fish with pasta so if the scallops or clams are large it is advisable to halve or quarter them.

> 100 ml olive oil
> 1 tablespoon celery, finely chopped
> 4 cloves garlic, finely chopped
> 2 tablespoons parsley, finely chopped
> black pepper, freshly ground
> 500 g scallops (reserve the coral for another dish)
> 300 g clams
> 2 tablespoons white wine
> pasta (p.84)

Heat the olive oil over high heat and add the celery, garlic, parsley and pepper. Cook until the garlic is golden brown. Reduce the heat to a low flame and add the scallops stirring them quickly to avoid catching. In a few minutes the scallops will be semi-cooked. Add the clams and wine and cook for a further four to five minutes still over slow heat. Serve at once with pasta of your choice.

Salsa di cozze/salsa di vongole

Mussel sauce/clam sauce

Both mussels and clams have, until recently, been little appreciated in Australia. Each works well in this sauce but if you use mussels cut the larger ones in half once you have taken them out of their shells. This sauce is also very good used in **risotto**.

> 100 ml olive oil
> 1 kg mussels or 1 kg clams, cleaned and thoroughly
>   scrubbed
> 2 cloves garlic, crushed
> 1 small onion, finely chopped
> 4 anchovy fillets, finely chopped
> 1 kg tomatoes, peeled and deseeded if fresh, or sieved
>   if tinned
> salt
> black pepper, freshly ground
> 1 tablespoon parsley, finely chopped
> pasta (p.84)

Heat the mussels or clams in 50 ml of the oil in a pan over a very high flame until the shells begin to open. Remove from the heat and as soon as the mussels or clams are cool enough to handle remove them from their shells. Discard any that are inferior. Reserve the liquid which the mussels or clams have exuded while being opened. Cut any large mussels in half.

Heat the remaining 50 ml of oil in a saucepan and lightly brown the garlic and onion. Add the liquid from the mussels or clams and bring to the boil. Moderate the heat and cook until the liquid has reduced. Stirring well with the addition of each ingredient, add the anchovies, tomatoes, salt and pepper. Boil, covered, for about ten minutes. The sauce will now be quite thick. Add the mussels or clams and parsley. Stir well and cook for a minute or two longer.

Serve immediately with a long, absorbent pasta.

Salsa di acciughe

Anchovy sauce

This quick and simple sauce is traditionally served on Easter Eve in Italy. It is best served with an absorbent, long pasta and when planning the rest of your menu remember that the anchovy flavour in this sauce is strong and dominating.

> 1 tin anchovy fillets
> 4 cloves garlic, whole
> 100 ml olive oil, including the oil from the anchovies
> pasta (p.84)

Remove the eyes from each end of the garlic and skewer each clove diagonally with two toothpicks.

Put all the ingredients together in a saucepan and cook over a low flame until the garlic is golden and the anchovies have had time to amalgamate with the oil. Remove the garlic. Toss the pasta gently in the sauce when it is ready and serve immediately.

Salsa di seppia

Cuttlefish sauce

This sauce is also known as **salsa con seppia alla Riminese**, *after the port of Rimini where it is a popular dish. Squid can be substituted for cuttlefish if necessary.*

50 g butter
75 ml olive oil
30 g onion, finely chopped
1 clove garlic, crushed
1 small hot red chilli (optional), finely chopped
300 g cuttlefish, cleaned, washed and cut into rings
150 ml dry white wine
500 g tomatoes, peeled and deseeded if fresh, or
    sieved if tinned
salt
black pepper, freshly ground
pasta (p.84)

Heat the butter and oil in a large saucepan and fry the onion, garlic and chilli until golden brown. Take care that the butter does not burn. Increase the heat, and add the cuttlefish, stirring continuously for two minutes. Add the wine, moderate the heat and let the wine reduce. Add the tomatoes, salt and pepper to taste and cook covered for thirty minutes, stirring occasionally.

Serve this sauce with a thick pasta such as *rigatoni*.

Salsa del pirata
Buccaneer's sauce

This sauce is sometimes called **salsa del pirata alla Genovese**, after the coastal region where it originated. It is very rich, and this goes some way to explaining its name. There was a belief that pirates lived in luxury and — at the end of their careers — could count on a generous last meal from their executioners.

> 100 ml olive oil
> 3 cloves garlic, crushed
> black pepper, freshly ground
> salt
> 500 g tomatoes, peeled and deseeded if fresh, or
>   sieved if tinned
> 100 g baby squid, cleaned and cut into thin strips
> 100 g prawns, shelled and cleaned thoroughly and
>   cut into bite-sized pieces
> 100 g fresh or tinned clams
> 1 tablespoon parsley, finely chopped
> pasta (p.84)

Heat 50 ml of the oil in a saucepan, add the garlic and lightly brown it. Add the pepper, salt and tomatoes and bring to the boil. Moderate the heat and cook uncovered for fifteen minutes.

Heat the remaining 50 ml of oil in another saucepan, add the squid and cook over a high flame for a few moments. Lower the flame and cook for ten minutes stirring occasionally. Add the prawns and clams and cook for five minutes. Stir in the tomato mixture and parsley and allow the sauce to simmer gently for a further ten minutes. Serve hot with a long absorbent pasta such as *spaghetti, trinetti* or *linguini*.

Salsa di tonno fresco oppure sgombri

Fresh tuna or mackerel sauce

This sauce is popular in the coastal areas of Italy especially around Genoa and in Sicily. Remember when you are preparing the fish fillets that they have to be eaten with a fork and with pasta and therefore should not be too big.

> 100 ml olive oil
> 3 cloves garlic, crushed
> black pepper, freshly ground
> salt
> 1 kg tomatoes, peeled and deseeded if fresh, or sieved
>   if tinned
> 1 kg fresh tuna or mackerel fillets
> 1 tablespoon flour
> a little extra oil
> 1 tablespoon parsley, finely chopped
> pasta (p.84)

Heat the oil in a saucepan and lightly brown the garlic. Add some black pepper, salt and the tomatoes and cook gently over a low flame for thirty minutes. Dust the fish fillets with flour and lightly fry them in a little oil. Add the fillets and the parsley to the tomatoes and cook for a further ten minutes. Serve immediately with any pasta of your choice.

Salsa di tonno in scatola

Tinned tuna sauce

This sauce is useful when fresh fish is not available. In Australia tinned tuna can be bought 'Italian style', that is, preserved in oil as well as tinned in brine. When preparing this sauce check which variety you are using; if the latter increase the quantity of oil in the recipe by 25-50 ml.

> 50 ml olive oil
> 1 small onion, finely chopped
> 2 cloves garlic, crushed
> 500 g tomatoes, peeled and deseeded if fresh, or
> sieved if tinned
> 1 bay leaf
> 1 350 g tin tuna
> 1 tablespoon parsley, finely chopped
> pasta (p.84)

Heat the oil in a saucepan and lightly brown the onion and garlic. Add the tomatoes and bay leaf and cook for five minutes. Flake the tuna with a fork and add it with the parsley and basil to the tomatoes. Simmer, uncovered for fifteen minutes. Serve with any pasta of your choice.

Maccheroncelli con sardine

Maccheroncelli with sardines

This is a slightly fussy dish to make but it's well worth the effort; you'll find that the ingredients blend well, without the sardine flavour becoming overpowering.

> 500 g fresh sardines, cleaned
> 40 g sultanas, soaked in water for a while
> 2 cloves garlic, crushed
> 1 tablespoon breadcrumbs
> 50 ml olive oil
> salt
> pepper
> 400 g *maccheroncelli* (a *spaghetti* type pasta which is hollow)

Wash the sardines. Remove their heads and tails. Cook them for a short time in boiling water. Strain and remove all bones. Lightly brown the garlic in a little oil, then discard it. Add the sardines over a moderate heat until they are a golden colour. Strain the sultanas and add them, and the breadcrumbs, to the sardines. Stir gently. Boil the pasta in salted water until *al dente*. Strain, mix the sardine sauce in delicately and serve.

Tagliatelle al caviale

Tagliatelle with caviar

This is a Venetian dish. Very delicate, refined and eye-catching, it is a little elaborate but well worth the preparation.

> 1 small jar black caviar (about 50 g)
> 1 small jar red caviar (about 50 g)
> 2 tablespoons butter
> 1 egg, hardboiled and chopped
> 150 ml cream
> juice of half a lemon
> 1 small glass vodka
> salt
> pepper
> 400 g *tagliatelle*

Cook the *tagliatelle* in boiling salted water until it is *al dente*. While the pasta is cooking, melt the butter in a saucepan, then add the cream, egg and vodka. As soon as this mixture starts to bubble, remove the pan from the heat. Mix the sauce with the strained *tagliatelle*, sprinkle with pepper and top with the two caviars and lemon juice, then serve.

Lasagne della nonna

Grandmother's lasagne

This is a recipe from Signora Milani, Tiberio Donnini's grandmother. It takes longer to prepare than any of the recipes in this collection but the rewards are proportional. The secret of good **lasagne** *is to make it high rather than wide so choose a deep-sided baking dish rather than a wide and shallow container.*

> 1 kg *lasagne* pasta
> 150 g *Parmigiano* cheese, freshly grated
>
> MEAT SAUCE
> 80 g butter
> 1 small onion, finely chopped
> 1 medium carrot, finely chopped
> 1 stick celery, finely chopped
> 600 g lean pork or veal or mixture of both, finely
>   chopped
> 1 sprig thyme (or pinch of powdered thyme)
> 1 bay leaf
> 1 tablespoon parsley, finely chopped
> 500 g tomatoes, peeled and deseeded if fresh,
>   or sieved if tinned
>
> BESCIAMELLA SAUCE
> 60 g butter
> 50 g flour
> 500 ml milk, warmed
> 2 tablespoons *Parmigiano* cheese, freshly grated

Preheat the oven to 350°F, 165°C.

First, prepare the meat sauce. Melt the butter in a saucepan and add the onion, carrot and celery and cook them until the onion is a golden colour, taking care that the butter does not burn. Add the meat and cook until it is nicely browned. Now add the aromatics and tomatoes and cook for thirty minutes over a medium heat, stirring occasionally.

While the meat sauce is cooking, prepare the *besciamella*.

Melt the butter in a saucepan. Add the flour, and make a roux and cook gently for five minutes, taking care that it does not brown. Have the milk warmed and pour it on to the roux, whisking with a balloon whisk to prevent lumps forming. Simmer very slowly, stirring from time to time for thirty minutes. When the sauce is quite thick and has finished cooking add the *Parmigiano* cheese and mix it in well.

While you are waiting for the two sauces to finish cooking, cook the *lasagne* pasta. Have a large pot of boiling salted water, to which you have added 1 tablespoon of oil or butter. Stand a pot of cold water nearby. Cook four or five squares of pasta at a time in the boiling water until they are *al dente*. Take each sheet out of the boiling water with tongs, plunge it into the cold water and then drain and lay on a clean tea towel until the remaining pasta is ready.

Choose a deep-sided baking dish and oil the bottom of it with a little oil from the top of the saucepan holding the meat sauce.

When both sauces and the pasta are cooked you can finish preparing the *lasagne*. Put a layer of pasta on the bottom, then a layer of *besciamella*, a layer of meat sauce and a sprinkle of freshly grated *Parmigiano*. Repeat this until all the ingredients are used. As you build up the layers remember to alternate the line of direction of the pasta sheets and to keep the layers of sauce sparse. Allow the sheets of pasta to flange up the sides of the baking dish.

When you have finished constructing the *lasagne* top it with a thin layer of the oil remaining from the meat sauce. Now tuck the *lasagne* into the dish with a wooden spoon by pushing the sheets of pasta down around the edges of the dish. It's much the same procedure as 'tucking in' a baby.

Finally top with a few dots of butter and the remaining *Parmigiano* and bake for thirty minutes. Serve hot.

Pasticcio di maccheroni

Baked macaroni

This macaroni dish can be used as a substitute for **lasagne**. It is similar but takes less time to prepare. The pasta used can be macaroni or you can use this recipe as a vehicle for using up leftover quantities of any pasta you have to hand, say, **rigatoni**.

600 g *maccheroni*
300 g mushrooms, wiped clean and finely sliced

BOLOGNESE MEAT SAUCE
Follow the method on pp.134-5 using the following
 ingredients:
50g butter
50 ml olive oil
1 onion, finely sliced
1 stalk celery, finely chopped
1 medium carrot, finely chopped
100 g *pancetta* or *prosciutto* (or bacon),
 finely chopped
200 g lean pork, minced
200 g lean veal, minced
50 g continental sausage, skinned and minced
½ glass dry white wine
500 g tomatoes, peeled and deseeded if fresh, or
 sieved if tinned

BESCIAMELLA SAUCE
Follow the method on p.127 using the following
 quantities:
50 g butter
50 g flour
500 ml milk, warmed
1 tablespoon *Parmigiano* cheese, freshly grated

Prepare the Bolognese sauce and enrich it with the mushrooms. Prepare the *besciamella*.

Boil the pasta (p.84) in salted water until *al dente*. Drain it well and mix it with the *Bolognese* and *besciamella* sauces. Place the mixture into an ovenproof dish pre-coated with butter mixed with breadcrumbs. Cover with freshly grated *Parmigiano* cheese and bake in a pre-heated oven (350°F, 165°C) for thirty minutes.

Rigatoni all'oregano

Rigatoni with oregano

This is not a dish with a long history, dating from the eighteenth or nineteenth centuries and being a typical sauce of Naples.

> 2 small *mozzarella* cheeses
> 500 g tomatoes, peeled and deseeded if fresh, or
> sieved if tinned
> 1 tablespoon oregano
> 4 cloves garlic, finely chopped
> 75 ml olive oil
> sugar
> salt
> pepper, freshly ground
> 400 g *rigatoni*

Lightly brown the garlic in the olive oil. Add tomatoes and a pinch of sugar, salt and pepper. Stir, then cover and simmer over a low heat for twenty minutes. Then add the oregano. Cook the *rigatoni* in boiling salted water until it is *al dente*. Cut the *mozzarella* cheeses into small cubes. Strain the pasta and mix it with the oregano sauce. Top with *mozzarella* cubes and serve.

Rigatoni al forno

Baked rigatoni

This dish is similar to **lasagne** and to the **pasticcio di maccheroni** but it is much more economical to prepare.

> 600 g rigatoni (half cooked)
> 100 ml olive oil
> 1 small onion, finely chopped
> 2 cloves garlic, finely chopped
> 1 kg tomatoes, peeled and deseeded if fresh, or sieved
>   if tinned
> salt
> black pepper, freshly ground
> 100 g *salami*, sliced
> 200 g *mozzarella*, finely chopped
> *pecorino* cheese, freshly grated
> 2 extra tomatoes, sliced (4 tomatoes if tinned)
> 3 tablespoons breadcrumbs
> extra oil

Pre-heat the oven to 350°F, 165°C.

Heat the oil in a saucepan and lightly brown the onion and garlic. Add the tomatoes, salt and pepper. Bring to the boil, moderate the heat and simmer for thirty minutes.

Butter a casserole and sprinkle with a thin layer of breadcrumbs. Put a layer of semi-cooked *rigatoni* on the bottom of the dish. Cover with a little of the prepared tomato sauce, a few slices of *salami, mozzarella* and a sprinkle of *pecorino*. Repeat the layers until all the ingredients are used. Top with slices of tomato and then cover with a light sprinkling of breadcrumbs with a little oil drizzled over. Bake for thirty minutes.

Cannelloni Eros

This sauce is named after Signora Eros Milani, Tiberio Donnini's grandmother.

> 12 *cannelloni* (bought in advance)
> 500 g fresh *ricotta* cheese
> 150 g *Parmigiano* cheese, freshly grated
> 2 tablespoons parsley, finely chopped
> salt
> *salsa di pomodoro* (pp.84-5)
> *besciamella* sauce (p.127)
> butter

Thoroughly mix the *ricotta*, 100 grams of the *Parmigiano* cheese, the chopped parsley and a pinch of salt together in a bowl. Spoon about two tablespoons of this mixture into each of the *cannelloni* and place them neatly in a buttered casserole. Cover the *cannelloni* with the *salsa di pomodoro* and then with the *besciamella* and the remaining 50 g of *Parmigiano* cheese. Dot the surface with a little butter and place in a pre-heated oven (400°F, 205°C) for twenty to twenty-five minutes.

Maccheroni imbottiti

Filled macaroni

Similar to **cannelloni** *but far more economical to make, this recipe uses jumbo* **maccheroni** *made without eggs and is a substantial and filling dish. The filling for the* **maccheroni** *can be made from any balanced combination of ingredients you have to hand and it is a good vehicle for using up leftovers.*

600 g jumbo *maccheroni* (cooked in advance for about four minutes or so that it is semi-cooked; drain and rinse in cold water)

FILLING
75 ml olive oil
1 small onion, finely chopped
500 g lean pork, finely chopped
salt
black pepper, freshly ground
100 g *mortadella* sausage, finely chopped
80 g *provolone* cheese, freshly grated
80 g *mozzarella* cheese, finely chopped

SAUCE
75 ml olive oil
2 cloves garlic, finely chopped
1 small onion, finely chopped
1½ kg tomatoes, peeled and deseeded if fresh, or
    sieved if tinned
salt
black pepper, freshly ground
120 g *pecorino* cheese, freshly grated

Preheat the oven to 350°F, 165°C.
    To make the filling, heat the olive oil in a saucepan and lightly brown the onion. Add the pork, salt and pepper and cook over moderate heat for five to seven minutes, stirring

from time to time. Remove from the heat and put the mixture aside to cool.

To make the sauce heat a further 75 ml of oil in another saucepan and lightly brown the onion and garlic. Add the tomatoes, salt and pepper and simmer for about 30 minutes.

Once the pork has cooled add the *mortadella, provolone* and *mozzarella* and mix thoroughly. Fill the half-cooked *maccheroni* with this mixture. It is easiest to do this by filling the pasta only from one end, allowing the air to escape from the other. As you fill each *maccheroni* put them neatly into a well-buttered casserole which you have sprinkled lightly with breadcrumbs to prevent the pasta sticking. As each layer of pasta is completed cover it with tomato sauce and sprinkle with *pecorino* cheese. Continue until all the ingredients are used finishing with a layer of tomato sauce and *pecorino* cheese. Bake for twenty-five to thirty minutes or until golden on top. Serve hot.

Salsa verde (cotta e cruda)

Green sauce (cooked and uncooked)

This is an excellent sharp green sauce used with **bollito misto** from which you have made the broth for **pasta in brodo** (pp. 46-8) or as an accompaniment to boiled or steamed fish or chicken. There are two interchangeable versions, cooked and uncooked.

> COOKED
> 75 ml olive oil
> 1 tablespoon parsley, finely chopped
> 1 small onion, finely chopped
> 150 g *giardineria* (mixed vegetables in vinegar), finely chopped
> 2 small green capsicums, finely chopped

Heat the oil in a frying pan, add the parsley and cook for one or two minutes. Add the onion and cook until golden brown. Add the *giardineria* and the green capsicum. Cook until the capsicum is soft.

At this point more oil can be added if necessary. As in all Italian cooking always start with a little oil and only add more as necessary to obtain the greatest nutritional value and flavour from the oil.

> UNCOOKED
> 2 cloves garlic
> 75 g breadcrumbs
> 1 tablespoon vinegar
> 125 ml olive oil
> 2 tablespoons parsley, finely chopped
> 1 hard boiled egg
> 150 g *giardineria*, finely chopped

Crush the garlic to a smooth paste, add the breadcrumbs, vinegar and oil and mix until all the ingredients have amalgamated. Add the parsley and the mashed egg yolk. Cut the white of the egg into fine strips and add it to the mixture with the *giardineria*.

INDEX

Amatriciana sauce 126
American sauce 133
anchovy: minestrone with anchovy 60,
  sauce 151, tomato and anchovy sauce 90
angel's hair pasta: with mushrooms 120,
  with smoked salmon 147
artichoke: pasta with 104, penne with 105

basil: sauce 92-3, soup 58, tomato and
  basil sauce 88
beans: broad beans with rice 79, broad
  beans and stockfish soup 71, kidney
  bean ragout 125, kidney bean sauce 124
beef broth 47, beef and chicken broth 47
Bolognese sauce 134-5
breadcrumb sauce 132
broad beans: with rice 79, bean and
  stockfish soup 71
broccoli: nymph's spaghetti 106, with
  short pasta 107, soup 67
broth 46-8, beef and chicken 47, chicken
  48, fish 48, gnocchetti in broth 74, with
  semolina 73, spinach gnocchetti in
  broth 75-6
Brussels sprout sauce 111
bucatini: with cheese and eggs 141, with
  julienne sauce 110
buccaneer's sauce 153
Burano sauce 148
bushman's sauce 121

Calabrese style penne 101
cannelloni Eros 163
capsicum and lamb sauce 136
Casinalbo macaroni 100
caviar, tagliatelle with 157
celery sauce 112
cheese 26, bucatini with eggs and cheese
  141, mozzarella sauce 131, pasta with
  ricotta 129, penne with four cheeses
  130, penne with pecorino and pepper
  130
chianti, rice with 78
chick pea soup 65
chicken: broth 48, sauce 137, liver sauce
  142, livers with tagliatelle 143
clam: sauce 150, clam and scallop sauce
  149

consommé with eggs 61
cream-based sauces: angel's hair with
  smoked salmon 147, fusilli with cream
  and ham 90, gorgonzola sauce 128,
  Modenese style sauce 138, mushroom
  sauce 22, spaghetti alla Carbonara 139,
  tagliatelle with caviar 157
cuttlefish sauce 152

dough, basic pasta 18-22

eggs: bucatini with cheese and eggs 141,
  consommé with eggs 61, 'torn' soup 63
eggplant, pasta with 114

fennel, spaghetti with 116
fettucine with onions 113
fish: broth 48, soup 72, sauces see pages
  147-156
fusilli with cream and ham 90

garlic 25, oil and garlic sauce 91
'good' sauce 99
gnocchetti in broth 74, spinach 75-6
gnocchi, potato 37-8
gnocco 43-4
gorgonzola sauce 128
green sauce 165-6

ham and cream with fusilli 90
herbs 25, soup 59

julienne sauce 110

kidney bean: sauce 124, ragout 125

lamb and capsicum sauce 136
lasagne, grandmother's 158-9
leeks with rice 80
lemon: soup 56, tomato and lemon sauce
  87

macaroni: baked 160-1, Casinalbo 100,
  filled 164-5, with marjoram 96, with
  olives 117
maccheroncelli with sardines 156
mackerel sauce 154
marjoram, macaroni with 96